Good Practice in
Child Care Cases

GOOD PRACTICE IN CHILD CARE CASES

A Guide for Solicitors Acting in Public Law Children Act
Proceedings Including Cases Involving Adoption

The Law Society

*With the Association of Lawyers for Children, Child Care Law Joint Liaison
Group and Solicitors Family Law Association*

The Law Society

© The Law Society 2004

ISBN 1 85328 961 2

Published by the Law Society in 2004
113 Chancery Lane
London WC2A 1PL

Typeset by J&L Composition, Filey, N. Yorks
Printed by TJ International Ltd, Padstow, Cornwall

Contents

Acknowledgements

Good Practice in Child Care Cases was drafted by the following:

Christina Blacklaws, *Law Society's Children Law Sub-Committee*

Graham Cole, *Child Care Law Joint Liaison Group*

Katherine Gieve, *Solicitors Family Law Association*

Liz Goldthorpe, *Association of Lawyers for Children*

Lynn Graham, *Legal Services Commission*

Rosemary Hanna, *Department for Constitutional Affairs*

Pat Monro, *Law Society's Children Law Sub-Committee*

Charles Prest, *CAFCASS*

Rachel Rogers, *Law Society*

Philip Thomson, *Law Society's Children Law Sub-Committee*

Joan Vis, *Solicitors Family Law Association*

Nabila Zulfiqar, *Child Care Law Joint Liaison Group*

Thanks are also given to the following for their assistance and contributions:

Richard Clark, *Child Care Law Joint Liaison Group*

Ellie Cronin, *Law Society*

Julie Hine, *CAFCASS*

Cheryl Morris, *Law Society*

Tim O'Regan, *Law Society's Children Law Sub-Committee*

Vanessa Richardson, *Child Care Law Joint Liaison Group*

William Simmonds, *Child Care Law Joint Liaison Group*

Richard White, *Law Society's Children Law Sub-Committee*

Foreword

by Dame Elizabeth Butler-Sloss, President of the Family Division

As all those involved in child care cases are aware, the issues that have to be resolved require the most careful and sensitive handling by the judges, magistrates, practitioners, and professionals coming into contact with the child and their family. All solicitors acting in these matters have a vital role to play in ensuring that cases are dealt with justly and fairly, with the minimum of distress to the children and individuals concerned.

The Law Society with the Association of Lawyers for Children, the Child Care Law Joint Liaison Group and the Solicitors Family Law Association are to be congratulated for producing this excellent good practice guide. It is an admirable supplement to the Law Society's *Family Law Protocol*. It is also a timely and welcome initiative further to the development of the Protocol for Judicial Case Management last year.

This publication provides practical and welcome guidance to solicitors who practise in this important, difficult and sensitive field and I am happy to endorse it.

Elizabeth Butler-Sloss
President of the Family Division

Preface

ABOUT *GOOD PRACTICE IN CHILD CARE CASES*

This book, published here for the first time, is a collection of concise good practice guidelines for all solicitors acting in public law Children Act cases, whether they are acting for a local authority, a parent, a child or another party. Other relevant guidance is appended.

- **Part 1** sets out the general principles that need to be considered by all solicitors, whichever party they act for.

- **Part 2** includes common issues that need to be considered by all solicitors involved in public law Children Act proceedings.

- **Part 3** deals in particular with the role of solicitors acting for local authority clients.

- **Part 4** deals with matters to be considered when instructed by children or children's guardians.

- **Part 5** outlines the approach to be taken by solicitors when acting for parents and other adult parties.

- **Part 6** covers good practice in relation to other aspects of public law children cases, including adoption.

The first five parts have been written with care order applications in mind, but are intended to be of general assistance with client and professional relationships, and the aspects of conduct covered will also be relevant for other types of specified proceedings.

The appendices include the Law Society's guidance on acting in the absence of a children's guardian (Appendix 8); and guidance issued jointly by the Law Society's Children Law Sub-Committee and CAFCASS on the working relationship between Children Panel solicitors and children's guardians (Appendix 10).

AIMS OF THIS GUIDE

1. To accompany the Law Society's *Family Law Protocol*, which does not cover public law cases involving children.

2. To provide supportive guidance on the conduct of cases and the particular approach required for less experienced practitioners who are not yet members of the Law Society's Children Panel, and an *aide mémoire* for more experienced practitioners.

3. To ensure the highest standards of representation for children and their families affected by public law Children Act proceedings, addressing the needs of the client.

4. To complement, but not duplicate, the Protocol for Judicial Case Management in Public Law Children Act Cases.

SCOPE

This book has been drafted by the Law Society's Children Law Sub-Committee with the Association of Lawyers for Children, the Child Care Law Joint Liaison Group (Association of Council Secretaries and Solicitors in Local Government) and the Solicitors Family Law Association, with the active support and close involvement of the Children and Family Court Advisory and Support Service, the Department for Constitutional Affairs and the Legal Services Commission. Consultation was also undertaken to ensure that the views of practitioners and other interested parties were taken into account. The intention is that it should form a benchmark of good practice with which all solicitors practising children law in England and Wales should comply.

Many experienced child care solicitors will undoubtedly find that they already practise to the standard outlined, but even they may find it a helpful guide. For those solicitors who are newly qualified or less experienced, there will be much in this document which will assist them in their professional development in the practice of public law children cases.

It is also hoped that members of the public and the judiciary will find it of assistance in indicating the expected standards to be practised by those representing or appearing before them.

This is the first edition of the guide. The intention is to update the document regularly to accommodate any changes in law and practice. Users of this document are encouraged to write to the Law Society with comments which will be of considerable help in reviewing this first edition.

PART 1

General principles

1.1   CHILD FOCUS

1.1.1   Solicitors must ensure that the principle that a child's interests are paramount is reflected in the conduct of the case itself. Solicitors acting for local authorities, for parents and other adult parties, or for the child or children's guardian, giving instructions on the child's behalf, all have a duty to act on the instructions of their particular client. Each client may have a different view on the child's interests. However, all solicitors can, and should, adopt a child-focused approach by ensuring that the presentation of their client's case takes into account the needs of the child throughout.

1.2   THE 'NON-ADVERSARIAL' APPROACH

1.2.1   Case law and guidance states that public law Children Act proceedings should be treated as 'non-adversarial'. This requires clarification given that such proceedings, by their nature, are clearly adversarial, as the evidence to satisfy the threshold criteria must be thoroughly tested. In practice, 'non-adversarial' means that solicitors should not behave in an unduly adversarial, aggressive or confrontational manner. All child care cases should be approached in a spirit of professional cooperation. All solicitors, whoever they are representing, should be committed to avoiding delay in the interests of the child. Solicitors have a duty to promote these principles in the interests of children and should bear in mind the following:

(a)   A child's development and timescale require prompt, effective decision-making using evidence relevant to that child's needs.

(b)   Children and their families are not usually involved in proceedings by choice.

(c)   The effect of proceedings on the child and members of the family can be profound, and long-term, particularly if the proceedings are acrimonious or badly managed. The actions of solicitors can in themselves, therefore, undermine the effectiveness of measures ordered by the court.

(d)   Proceedings can affect both the child's continuing relationship with the family and personal relationships within the family, as well as the local authority's ongoing professional relationship with the child and family.

1.2.2   Solicitors must therefore:

(a)   Avoid adopting an antagonistic or confrontational attitude in their approach to the case, or advocacy that may cause unnecessary acrimony, delay or cost. Solicitors should remember that if one party behaves in such a manner, the other parties may feel forced to do so. All solicitors should resist such an approach, however 'productive' this may appear to be in the short term.

(b)   Ensure that all parties and their legal representatives are treated with respect and that all matters are dealt with in as courteous and relaxed a manner as possible. (However, it is unprofessional to use first names in correspondence between solicitors.)

1.3   TESTING THE EVIDENCE

1.3.1   Solicitors must ensure that they rigorously test all the evidence, and advise their clients to concede issues and/or contest the case as appropriate, both in relation to the threshold criteria and all other evidence. Full consideration should always be given of the need to conduct cross-examinations on the evidence in a thorough but professional and courteous manner.

1.4 PROFESSIONAL APPROACH

1.4.1 Solicitors must take care not to become so involved in a case that their personal emotions or own emotional response to the child or any issue in the case adversely affect their judgement, retaining a professional and objective relationship with the client. Clients have the right to put their case and solicitors must be careful not to substitute their own judgement on what is in the child's best welfare interests for that of their client. In acting professionally solicitors should:

(a) Listen to the clients and take instructions throughout.

(b) Explain to clients the approach the court is likely to take and give them guidance.

(c) Advise clients carefully on the available options and likely outcomes on the basis of the evidence. Solicitors should ensure that they objectively evaluate the evidence, particularly at the early stages, so as, for example, to avoid unsuccessful applications for interim orders which serve only to cause unnecessary conflict and costs.

(d) Properly exercise professional judgement in advising clients when there are reasonable grounds to contest and when it is appropriate to compromise, reach an agreement or make concessions.

(e) Advise clients throughout on the consequences of their actions, including the consequences of failing to follow advice.

1.4.2 At the conclusion of proceedings, clients should be advised of their rights of appeal, if appropriate, but solicitors should not be carried away by the feelings of the client.

1.5   CASE MANAGEMENT AND AVOIDING DELAY

1.5.1   Solicitors have a duty, as the client's representative and as officers of the court, to ensure that all cases are dealt with in a proper manner, efficiently and effectively. Solicitors must therefore be proactive in managing cases, and make sure that wherever necessary, matters are returned to the court in a timely manner. The paramount objectives, unless the needs of the child dictate otherwise, must be to avoid delay and complete a case within a maximum of 40 weeks, as set by the Protocol for Judicial Case Management in Public Law Children Act Cases ('the Protocol'), applicable from 1 November 2003. The Protocol and all documents relating to the Protocol, including Standard Variable Directions, and Local Plans published for each care centre and Family Proceedings Court (containing valuable information and guidance as to the conduct of public law proceedings in that centre) are available at **www.courtservice.gov.uk/using_courts/protocol/index.htm**.

1.5.2   All child care proceedings should be dealt with expeditiously and solicitors should use their best endeavours to comply with directions made by the court, particularly with regard to the timetable. All solicitors must avoid delay and contribute to cooperative, timely and organised case management.

(a)   Solicitors must comply with the Protocol, so far as is practicable. The Protocol provides a common, timed framework for case management, in every case and at every stage and level. It sets out six steps and includes guidance and documentation for conduct in each of the steps. The overriding objective of the Protocol, as defined in *Practice Direction (Care Cases: Judicial Continuity and Judicial Case Management)* is attached at Appendix 2, and the Protocol's 'Route Map – The 6 Steps' is at Appendix 1.

(b)   Solicitors must remain aware that there may be cases where there is a need to adapt the procedure, for example where there are changes in circumstances or to allow for planned, purposeful, constructive delay in order to achieve the best possible outcome for the child.

(c) All solicitors, not only the child's solicitor, must be mindful of their role in case management and be prepared to contact the other parties or their representatives in an appropriate manner for the filing of documentation if necessary.

1.6 MENTORING

1.6.1 Difficult situations can arise in any child care case. Sources of formal and informal information and support are available. All solicitors should consider seeking advice from other members of the profession in and outside their firm or local authority legal department, including from members of the Law Society's Children Panel. The relevant practitioner associations can assist in finding professional mentors. Their contact details are contained in Appendix 11.

1.6.2 In cases where no guardian has been allocated for the child, it is a matter for individual solicitors to decide whether or not to accept an appointment as the child's solicitor, taking into account their ability and competence to act and with close regard to the child's best interests. All solicitors in this position should consider seeking the advice and support of a mentor or mentors and once appointed, should continue to seek their assistance and guidance until the children's guardian is allocated or an independent social worker is instructed.

1.7 GOOD PRACTICE GUIDANCE

1.7.1 Solicitors must comply with the rules and principles of conduct contained in *The Guide to the Professional Conduct of Solicitors 1999*, published by the Law Society. All references to the Guide in this good practice guide refer to the eighth edition, unless stated otherwise. The internet version is accessible at **www.guide-on-line.lawsociety.org.uk**.

1.7.2 The Law Society's Professional Ethics department can be contacted on 0870 606 2577 between 11 am and 1 pm, and between 2 pm and 4 pm. They can provide guidance concerning issues of professional conduct.

1.7.3 The SFLA has published a *Guide to Good Practice for Solicitors Acting for Children* (sixth edition, 2002). This is updated regularly. Copies are obtainable from the SFLA. Contact details are contained in Appendix 11. All solicitors should read this guide, which solicitors acting for children are recommended to observe.

1.7.4 A new, comprehensive handbook on good practice in child law, edited by Pat Monro and Liz Goldthorpe, is due to be published by Law Society Publishing in 2004.

PART 2

Common issues

2.1 HUMAN RIGHTS

2.1.1 Solicitors must have knowledge of the Human Rights Act 1998 (HRA 1998), relevant Strasbourg jurisprudence and case law arising, and must keep this knowledge up to date. Solicitors must have particular regard to the European Convention on Human Rights (ECHR), Article 6 (right to fair trial) and Article 8 (right to respect for family life). They should ensure that proceedings are conducted with due regard to such rights, for example in relation to delay, time for preparation, equality of arms, access to documentation and rehabilitation, and that any order sought regarding a child is 'legal and proportionate'.

2.1.2 Solicitors should not use HRA 1998 inappropriately to bolster weak cases or to bring inappropriate points, but they must carefully consider, and keep under review, the general issue as to whether clients' human rights have been breached. If so, solicitors should give advice to clients as to what further action should be taken.

2.1.3 The effects of HRA 1998 are not confined to the court process. Solicitors should be aware of the decisions in *Re M (Care: Challenging Decisions by the Local Authority)* [2001] 2 FLR 1300, *Re L (Care: Assessment: Fair Trial)* [2002] EWHC 1379 (Fam), [2002] 2 FLR 730 and *Re G (Care: Challenge to LA's Decision)* [2003] EWHC 551 (Fam), [2003] 2 FLR 42 in connection with ECHR, Articles 6 (right to fair trial) and 8 (right to respect for family life).

2.1.4   Solicitors should have knowledge of the United Nations Convention on the Rights of the Child 1989 available at **www.unhchr.ch** (click on the link for Treaties). This Convention has been ratified by the UK but does not have direct effect. However, international standards will become increasingly important. The Convention has been endorsed both by the European and domestic courts. It is endorsed by the Law Society and the authors of this guide.

2.1.5   Solicitors should observe the content of *Practice Direction (Family Proceedings: Human Rights)* [2000] 4 All ER 288.

2.2   DIVERSITY ISSUES

2.2.1   Solicitors should be sensitive to issues of ethnicity, language, religion, culture, gender and vulnerability, in relation to the child, their dealings with clients and the issues in each case.

2.2.2   Solicitors should consider the information needed by the court to address diverse cultural contexts. Local authority solicitors should seek to ensure that applications make clear at an early stage the family's race, language, culture and religion. It is important, in addition to providing the descriptive information, to bring to the court's attention the substantive relevance and significance, if any, of the cultural context in each particular case. Solicitors for all the parties should consider what directions are necessary to ensure that relevant evidence on culturally diverse contexts is available to the court.

2.2.3   Solicitors should also be sensitive to the services needed by disabled children and adults. For example:

(a)   Consider in advance access to the court room.

(b)   Consider additional services that might be offered in the context of the care plan and whether venues for therapeutic services are accessible by the child.

(c)   Check that contact venues are suitable for both the child and adults involved.

Any perceived need for special facilities should be made known to the court as soon as possible.

2.3 COMMUNICATION WITH OTHER PARTIES AND WITH CLIENTS

2.3.1 Solicitors must show courtesy and be professional in all communications with other solicitors or parties. Solicitors should not give personal opinions or comments within letters. Solicitors are referred to the SFLA's *Guide to Good Practice on Correspondence*, obtainable from the Solicitors Family Law Association (SFLA). Contact details are contained in Appendix 11. Where there are current proceedings with the local authority on the record, solicitors for non-local authority parties should not contact members of social services departments direct without the consent of the relevant local authority legal department (Guide, Principle 19.02), or in accordance with any relevant local authority policy. If this is not the case, it is good practice to attempt to notify the legal department before contacting the social services department, and to copy to both departments any written queries or correspondence directed to social services. In many instances, it may be of assistance to contact the legal department initially.

2.3.2 Where the solicitor for the child intends to visit the child in a local authority placement, to take instructions from an older child, for example, or where the child is not yet allocated a children's guardian, it is good practice to inform the local authority's legal department, and as a matter of courtesy to liaise with the social worker so that arrangements can be made with the extended family, foster carer or children's home. Local authority solicitors should encourage a facilitative approach to enabling solicitors to visit children.

2.3.3 It is good practice for a child's solicitor who is considering a visit to the child at home, where the child is still living at home, to contact the solicitor for the resident parent(s) as a matter of courtesy, and to discuss whether arrangements should be made with the parent(s) direct or through their solicitor.

2.3.4 Communications must focus on identification of issues and their resolution. They should be clear and free of jargon. Protracted, unnecessary, hostile and inflammatory exchanges and 'trial by correspondence' must be avoided. The effect of correspondence upon clients and other family members should be considered so that correspondence sent by solicitors does not further inflame emotions, antagonise or offend. Solicitors should be particularly vigilant when acting for children to maintain even-handedness in correspondence with adult parties and their solicitors, and the local authority.

2.3.5 The impact of any correspondence upon its readers and in particular the parties including the child, must always be considered. It is crucial that solicitors or parties do not raise irrelevant issues nor unreasonably cause other parties or their own clients to adopt an entrenched, polarised or hostile position.

2.3.6 Where writing to unrepresented adult parties, solicitors should recommend that they seek independent legal advice and enclose a second copy of the letter to be passed to any solicitor instructed.

2.3.7 Solicitors are warned that they should not use email as a sole means of correspondence with other solicitors. Email should not be used to correspond with clients unless the client has given an express assurance that it is a suitable means of correspondence. Solicitors are advised to consult the Law Society's 'Guidance for Solicitors on the Use of Electronic Mail' (April 2000), noting that a revised edition will be available by early 2004, and 'Professional Ethics and IT' (June 2000). These are both available from Professional Ethics on 0870 606 2577. Use of email or text may be appropriate for communicating some matters to child clients if the child has access to these mediums and would like this method of communication to be used. However, the child must know that this might be used as a means of communication and be warned of the security risk, and a written record should be kept by their solicitor of all communications sent and received.

2.4 DOMESTIC ABUSE

2.4.1 Solicitors must be aware of the possible consequences to the welfare of the child and other family members wherever the issue of domestic abuse is raised.

2.4.2 Domestic abuse is often a significant factor in child protection cases. Solicitors are referred to the Law Society's *Family Law Protocol*, Part VI for guidance, for example on screening for domestic abuse and safety planning, including keeping parties' whereabouts confidential and preparing for safety issues within the court building. Local authority solicitors should be mindful of any need to keep a party's whereabouts confidential from another party on preparing the application.

2.4.3 Solicitors are reminded of the court's power to include an exclusion requirement in an interim care order under the Children Act 1989, s.38A.

2.4.4 Solicitors for adult parties should advise their clients as appropriate about the making of applications under the Family Law Act 1996, Part IV during the course of the public law proceedings. Solicitors must remain alert to safety issues for their client and any other children after removal of a child from the home.

2.5   CHILD PROTECTION CONFERENCES

2.5.1 Solicitors should read and observe the guidance issued by the Law Society's Family Law Committee, 'Attendance of Solicitors at Child Protection Conferences' (June 1997), available in the family law specialism section at **www.lawsociety.org.uk**. This guidance, however, does require some revision, which will be issued separately to this publication.

2.5.2 Child protection procedures, including the conduct of the child protection conference, are currently the responsibility of local Area Child Protection Committees acting in accordance with the Department of Health guidance contained in 'Working Together to Safeguard Children' (1999).

2.5.3 Local authority solicitors should remind social workers to recognise the role of solicitors for parents and other family members in the context of child protection procedures, and advise them to make information available on legal advice and assistance where the parents have not instructed a solicitor. Information on how to access information about finding a solicitor, including Children Panel members, is given at Appendix 3.

2.5.4 There may be value in a local authority solicitor attending child protection conferences to advise conference chairs on issues that may arise in connection with the running of the meeting, rather than on the child protection plan or the case.

2.5.5 Solicitors should expect child protection conferences to be conducted in a non-adversarial and respectful manner. If this is not the experience, it should be raised in the conference with the chair.

2.5.6 Although not a member, the local authority solicitor is part of the conference and solicitors acting for other parties cannot object to the local authority solicitor being present, even if their clients are there and they themselves are unable to attend. Child protection case conferences can be very difficult for parents. Solicitors for parents should consider accompanying their clients to such conferences to give them legal advice wherever possible and to try to arrange for attendance if they themselves are unavailable. It is important both to advise on the process of possible child protection registration and to gain background information to assist with the preparation of the client's case in connection with possible public law Children Act proceedings. However, the child protection case conference should not be used as a pre-trial review of a care case.

2.5.7 In September 2000, the Child Care Law Joint Liaison Group highlighted to local authority lawyers in particular, in their guidance 'Arrangements for Handling Child Care Cases' (available under the family law specialism section at **www.lawsociety. org.uk**) that where other parties (normally parents) are present, the local authority solicitor should not use their ability to attend, without the other party's solicitor being present, to unfair advantage.

2.6 FAMILY GROUP CONFERENCES

2.6.1 Solicitors should be aware of non-court based processes which may assist them to run the case, particularly the role of family group conferences. The family group conference is a growing area of social work practice, which can be a useful tool to avoid the issue of proceedings, or be recommended by the court to take place during the course of proceedings, where appropriate.

2.6.2 Family group conferences are a decision making forum that focus on the welfare of the child. At a family group conference, the wider family (this can include friends), meets and is given information by the relevant agencies on the needs of the child and the reasons why a decision is required. Members of the wider family are given time on their own to make a decision that promotes and safeguards the child's welfare. In care proceedings, family group conferences may be helpful:

(a)   in identifying family and community supports, so that it is safe for a child to live with his or her parent(s);

(b)   in identifying a placement in the wider family, if the child cannot live with his or her parent(s);

(c)   where a kinship placement is not possible, allowing the wider family to support the plan for the child.

Further information on the process is available on **www.frg.org.uk**.

2.6.3 Adult clients should be strongly advised and encouraged to attend any family group conference. Solicitors should have regard to family members or family friends who have not been invited yet may have something to contribute.

2.7   PUBLIC FUNDING AND COSTS INFORMATION

2.7.1 Solicitors are reminded of their professional duty to consider and advise clients on the availability of public funding where clients might be entitled to such assistance. In public law Children Act cases certain parties are entitled to non-means, non-merits tested legal representation for 'special Children Act proceedings' (other than appeal proceedings) under the Access to Justice Act 1999 Funding Code, para. 2.2, as follows:

'where Legal Representation is applied for on behalf of:

(i)   a child in respect of whom an application is made for an order under –

(a)   Section 31 (a care or supervision order);

(b)   Section 43 (a child assessment order);

(c) Section 44 (an emergency protection order); and

(d) Section 45 (extension or discharge of an emergency protection order);

(ii) any parent of such a child or person with parental responsibility for the child within the meaning of the 1989 Act;

(iii) a child who is brought before a court under Section 25 (use of accommodation for restricting liberty) who is not, but wishes to be, legally represented before the court.'

Legal representation for 'other public law children cases' as defined at para. 2.2 of the Funding Code (see *Legal Services Commission Manual* ('LSC Manual'), vol. 3, p.3A-19) including adoption and proceedings under the inherent jurisdiction of the High Court in relation to children, is subject to the means test and other criteria at para. 11.9 of the Funding Code (LSC Manual, vol. 3, p.3A-36).

2.7.2 Solicitors should note the guidance on over-representation at para. 20.16(2)(b) (LSC Manual, vol. 3, p.3C-165) and remember that where there is no conflict of interest sufficient to justify separate representation (by separate solicitor and/or counsel), it may be appropriate for one of the solicitors involved to represent the funded clients, and/or for there to be joint instruction of counsel. Failure to consider this may lead to unnecessarily duplicated costs being disallowed.

2.7.3 'Legal Help' and 'General Family Help' are available for public law children cases subject to the usual eligibility and other Funding Code criteria. However, General Family Help will only be appropriate where it can be used to negotiate with the local authority (see guidance on attendance at case conferences, para. 20.8(3), LSC Manual, vol. 3, p.3C-153).

2.7.4 Legal Help can be provided to a child client direct where the work is in relation to proceedings which the child is entitled to begin, prosecute or defend without a next friend or guardian *ad litem*. A child is for these purposes a person under 16 (see para. 2.3, LSC Manual, vol. 2, p.2A-83). Solicitors should also be aware that applications on behalf of a child may be made by:

(a) a parent, guardian or other person in whose care the child is;

(b)   a person acting for the purposes of any proceedings as the child's next friend or guardian *ad litem*;

(c)   any other person, where there is good reason why none of the above can apply and there is sufficient connection between the child and the other person to ensure that the other person is likely to act responsibly in the interests of the child, and the other person has sufficient knowledge of the child, the problem and the child's financial circumstances to give proper instructions (see para. 2.4, LSC Manual, vol. 2, p. 2A-83).

Note also that direct instructions can be accepted where there is good reason why any of the people referred to is unable to seek advice on the child's behalf, and the child is old enough to give instructions and understand the nature of funded legal advice.

2.7.5   Solicitors are reminded of their obligation to comply with the Solicitors' Costs Information and Client Care Code 1999 (see Solicitors' Practice Rules 1990, Rule 15). A serious breach of this Code, or persistent breaches of a material nature, could be treated as professional misconduct and/or inadequate professional services.

2.7.6   In particular, in accordance with the Solicitors' Costs Information and Client Care Code 1999, solicitors must generally:

(a)   Give clients the best information possible about the likely overall costs, including a breakdown between fees, VAT and disbursements, and the basis of charging. (It is recognised that such an estimate may need to be in broad terms at the commencement of a case and that the best information possible about the cost of the next stage of the matter may be given).

(b)   Discuss with clients how, when and by whom any costs are to be met and consider whether clients may be eligible for public funding.

(c)   Discuss with clients, and keep in mind at all times, the principle of proportionality between the likely outcome and the probable expense of resolving the dispute, having regard also to the impact of any possible costs orders.

(d)   Keep clients regularly updated about the level of costs.

However, in a publicly funded case where the client is not required to make a contribution and can have no potential costs liability, solicitors do not need to show that costs information has been given (see Solicitors' Costs Information and Client Care Code 1999, para. 2(d), and Specialist Quality Mark Standard, F1.1, 'Recording and offering confirmation of basic information'). Similarly, costs implications of the instruction of counsel would not need to be discussed. Nonetheless, solicitors must approach funded cases in the same way as if they were acting for private clients (Access to Justice Act 1999, s.22(4)) and must seek to obtain value for money for the Community Legal Service Fund as they would for a private client.

2.7.7   When clients are publicly funded, solicitors need to be aware of the requirements of public funding, and in particular must ensure clients are aware that there are circumstances in which solicitors' duties when undertaking publicly funded work can override their duty of client confidentiality. The solicitor is required to make a report to the Legal Services Commission (LSC), for example, where there is a belief that the publicly funded client requires the case to be conducted unreasonably or at an unjustifiable expense to the Community Legal Service Fund, or where the solicitor is simply uncertain as to whether it would be reasonable to continue acting. Costs may be disallowed following a failure to report and it is important that the client should be aware of this. Solicitors are referred to the Legal Services Commission (Disclosure of Information) Regulations 2000 (SI 2000/442), reg. 4, as amended (see LSC Manual, vol. 1, p.1B–74 and Principle 5.03 of the Guide).

2.7.8   In publicly funded proceedings, solicitors are obliged to inform a child client (who is instructing the solicitor direct rather than through a children's guardian) of technical matters such as their obligations to the LSC. It will be for the solicitor to judge if it is appropriate to send letters to the child client in the terms usually required. Similarly, solicitors should consider giving their address as the correspondence address for the child client – the solicitor is the child's agent for funding purposes (Funding Code Procedures, C9.4). If a particular public funding requirement is not going to be met, it is important to note this on the file with reasons, and if in doubt to clarify the situation with the LSC.

2.7.9 Solicitors are reminded of their duty to safeguard public funds and to ensure that the Funding Code criteria applicable to the case remain satisfied, although the criteria applied to 'special Children Act proceedings' (see para. 2.7.1 above) are limited. Solicitors must ensure that they file and serve Notice of Issue of a Certificate of Public Funding and Notice of Discharge of that certificate.

2.7.10 Solicitors should be aware of the Funding Code, Funding Code Procedures and the LSC decision-making guidance (see the LSC Manual, vol. 3) including the grant of legal representation, related proceedings, and extent of cover. They should also be aware that the children's guardian must look to CAFCASS rather than the LSC in the event of a conflict with the child. Professional guardians cannot apply for public funding (Funding Code Procedures, C3.3).

2.7.11 It is possible that the LSC will discharge a certificate granted on a non-means, non-merits tested basis, but this is unlikely given the nature of the proceedings. Where the discharge of such a certificate has to be considered, in particular where a client withdraws instructions and does not seek a change of solicitor, solicitors are advised to notify the LSC of the situation and as to whether in fact they should remain on the record, in order to avoid delay caused by the parent reappearing at a late stage seeking representation.

2.7.12 The LSC gave guidance in *Focus 40* (December 2002) to the effect that it may meet the costs of independent social work arising out of the delay in allocation of a children's guardian by CAFCASS, but that any payment will be limited to CAFCASS rates. Solicitors will have to justify any additional work undertaken due to the lack of a CAFCASS guardian.

2.7.13 As a matter of law, solicitors should not instruct experts without leave of the court. The LSC's view is that the local authority should meet the costs of Framework assessment work to support the care plan and assessments under Children Act 1989, s.38(6). Otherwise apportionment, where it is appropriate, should in the LSC's view be on a moiety (50/50) basis between the local authority and the funded parties rather than an equal basis between all the parties. The LSC advises that the solicitor should not agree apportionments for incorporation in court orders unless they are in line with the above. The solicitor should also be aware that the Community Legal Service Fund cannot meet the costs of treatment, therapy or training nor the client's subsistence expenses. The LSC expects the solicitor to obtain value for money: this may involve approaching more than one expert – see *Focus 41* (April 2003), followed up in *Focus 42* (July 2003). The LSC has, in the context of the implementation of the Protocol, issued an information pack regarding its position. This includes an item from *Focus 43* (October 2003), and solicitors may find it useful for both information and reference. The pack can be accessed at **www.legalservices.gov.uk** under Guidance, CLS Funded Work, or at **www.courtservice.gov.uk/using_courts/protocol/index.htm**.

2.7.14 Solicitors should note that applying for prior authority for disbursements is discretionary, rather than mandatory: see Civil Legal Aid (General) Regulations 1989, (SI 1989/339), reg. 61, as amended (LSC Manual, vol. 1, p.1B-90). Following the implementation of the Protocol, the LSC will follow court orders giving leave to instruct experts and to apportion their fees on the basis that the court has fully considered the issues in accordance with the Protocol and the Code of Guidance for Expert Witnesses in Family Proceedings (included in the Protocol as Appendix C). Where the Protocol has been followed, it is not necessary to apply for authority and to do so may serve only to delay the instruction of the expert and therefore the progress of the case.

2.7.15 Solicitors should be familiar with Civil Legal Aid (General) Regulations 1989 (SI 1989/339), reg. 101(1)(a) as amended (LSC Manual, vol. 1, p.1B–92). This allows for a payment on account of a disbursement, incurred or to be incurred, and in cases of joint instruction which are subject to the Protocol there is a unified application process. The lead solicitor can use Claim Form 4 to apply for a payment on behalf of all the funded clients in the case: the appropriate share of the expenditure is then paid to each firm involved and the expert can be paid without delay.

2.8   EXPERTS

2.8.1   So far as is practicable, solicitors must observe the Code of Guidance for Expert Witnesses in Family Proceedings (Appendix C of the Protocol at **www.courtservice.gov.uk/ using_courts/protocol/index.htm**) in relation to the use of experts and experts' meetings. The LSC's information pack referred to in para. 2.7.13 above provides useful information.

2.8.2   The court may need certain expertise or information before being in a position to make a decision in the case. The key issues for solicitors to consider at the earliest possible stage are:

(a)   what evidence is necessary;

(b)   whether additional evidence to that usually filed by the parties is necessary;

(c)   which party or parties should seek the evidence;

(d)   who should provide it.

Under the Protocol, the particular issue upon which expert evidence is required to assist the court must be defined.

2.8.3   All solicitors should bear in mind the possible sources of information. In order to avoid cost and delay, solicitors should consider whether anyone involved in the case has the necessary appropriate expertise to assist the court. This is likely to be the social services department or the children's guardian, particularly where social work expertise is required.

2.8.4   Solicitors should consider the specific field of knowledge required by the court, for example, expertise in adult or child psychiatry, paediatrics, or radiology before proposing to instruct an expert. A list of types of experts is at Appendix 4.

2.8.5   All solicitors should therefore ask themselves the following key questions:

(a)   Is an expert actually needed on particular issues?

(b)   What type of expert is required?

(c)   Could an assessment be obtained from an expert witness already involved in the case?

Appendix C, para. 2.3 of the Protocol makes it clear that any party who proposes to ask the court for permission to instruct an expert must set out why the expert evidence proposed cannot be given by social services, undertaking a core assessment, or by the children's guardian, in accordance with their different statutory duties.

2.8.6 Permission from the court must be sought before an expert is appointed. Solicitors should advise clients that they should not obtain experts' reports without prior permission from the court. Experts should only be instructed and their evidence only admitted where necessary: that is, in cases where other available evidence does not deal with the relevant issue and where the welfare of the child dictates that such further evidence ought to be obtained.

2.8.7 Recent and relevant experience on the part of the expert is essential. An expert who has a treatment role for a party should not be instructed to provide an independent expert report to the court.

2.8.8 Parties should be encouraged to use a single expert to be jointly instructed, if this is appropriate in the circumstances of the case. The costs of such an expert should be apportioned between the parties. When clients are publicly funded, solicitors must report to the LSC if clients will not agree to the use of a single expert where that would be appropriate to the case.

2.8.9 Solicitors for all parties should, however, recognise the need for evidence by different parties for different purposes, and the need of an individual party to have the opportunity to challenge expert evidence.

2.8.10 Letters of instruction to experts, whether agreed or not, are disclosable. Letters of instruction should be prepared in accordance with the Protocol, Appendix C, para. 3.1. They should appear in the court bundle. The letter should also ask the expert to advise as to whether the report or any part of it should be withheld from a party or parties, and if so, why.

2.8.11 Solicitors need to be aware of the provisions of the Guide, Principle 16.02, Note 5 and their duty to disclose experts' reports in proceedings under the Children Act 1989:

'5. In proceedings under the Children Act 1989 solicitors are under a duty to reveal experts' reports commissioned for the purposes of proceedings, as these reports are not privileged. The position in relation to voluntary disclosure of other documents or solicitor/client communications is uncertain. Clearly advocates are under a duty not to mislead the court (see 21.01, p.374). Therefore, if an advocate has certain knowledge which he or she realises is adverse to the client's case, the solicitor may be extremely limited in what can be stated in the client's favour. In this situation, the solicitor should seek the client's agreement for full voluntary disclosure for three reasons:

(i) the matters the client wants to hide will probably emerge anyway;

(ii) the solicitor will be able to do a better job for the client if all the relevant information is presented to the court;

(iii) if the information is not voluntarily disclosed, the solicitor may be severely criticised by the court.

If the client refuses to give the solicitor authority to disclose the relevant information, the solicitor is entitled to refuse to continue to act for the client if to do so will place the solicitor in breach of his or her obligations to the court.'

Solicitors should also advise clients of the above.

2.8.12 Solicitors are reminded to observe the Guide, Principle 20.01 in relation to the payment of experts' fees, including Note 4 on publicly funded cases.

2.9   PROFESSIONALS' MEETINGS

2.9.1 There are many types of professionals' meetings with which solicitors may be involved in the course of public law children work.

2.9.2 Solicitors must be clear about the nature and purpose of any meeting and their role at that meeting. A 'professionals' meeting' is a generic term and may mean different things to different professionals. Meetings include:

(a) an initial child protection conference;

(b)   a child protection conference to review a Child Protection Register decision;

(c)   an experts' discussion (meeting) in accordance with the Code of Guidance for Expert Witnesses in Family Proceedings (Protocol, Appendix C);

(d)   a professionals' meeting as envisaged by the Protocol: between the local authority and named professionals, probably non-lawyer professionals, for the purpose of assisting with local authority planning;

(e)   meeting as a case management tool to ascertain whether there is possible agreement on threshold, the outstanding issues, and the expert and other witnesses needed. This is likely to be an advocates' meeting as directed by the Protocol, but on occasions it may be appropriate and justified for the solicitors in the case to convene other professionals' meetings between lawyers only, or between lawyers and the social worker and the children's guardian, with or without lay client(s) present.

2.9.3   Where there is any preliminary meeting between the expert(s), social worker and children's guardian, solicitors should insist that this be minuted and the minutes disclosed to all parties.

2.9.4   Solicitors should keep in mind the value of suggesting an appropriate professionals' meeting in cases at not too late a stage.

2.9.5   In relation to all professionals' meetings, one solicitor should take lead responsibility for coordination, including preparing an agreed agenda in advance, and making advance arrangements for minutes to be taken and agreed. In practice it is often the child's solicitor who takes lead responsibility for coordination and chairing of professionals' meetings. The legal representatives of the other parties are entitled to be present.

2.10   CONTINUITY OF CONDUCT OF CASE

2.10.1   Clients must be given details of who is handling their case in accordance with the Solicitors' Costs Information and Client Care Code 1999 (see Solicitors' Practice Rules 1990, Rule 15).

It is desirable for the same solicitor to retain conduct of the case, wherever possible, particularly in relation to meetings with the client, and including advocacy at case management type hearings and substantive hearings where appropriate. Full and careful consideration should be given as to who will be the best advocate, in terms of serving the best interests of the client, to present the case at each case management hearing and at the final hearing.

2.10.2 Consistency of representation for the child is particularly important. All members of the Law Society's Children Panel are reminded of their undertaking included in Appendix 9.

2.11 THE USE OF COUNSEL OR SOLICITOR ADVOCATE

2.11.1 Where counsel or another solicitor advocate are involved, they must be adequately instructed. Briefs must include all material information, which will need to be considered by the court.

2.11.2 If the case is placed with counsel, they should have appropriate expertise in child care law. If the case is placed with another solicitor they should be a member of the Law Society's Children Panel, and approved as a children representative if representing the child, save in exceptional circumstances.

2.11.3 Solicitors should insist on the same counsel being retained throughout cases, and seek to obtain undertakings from them that they will take all reasonable steps to ensure that, so far as reasonably practicable, a conflicting professional arrangement does not arise that would stop them conducting the hearing. Again, Children Panel solicitors are reminded of the terms of their Children Panel undertaking to instruct another advocate when necessary or in the client's best interests.

2.11.4 Whenever another advocate is to appear on behalf of the client, the client must be aware, save in exceptional circumstances, of the identity of the advocate concerned. The solicitor conducting the case should discuss with the client the arrangements for attendance by a responsible representative of the solicitor with that advocate and the client. Solicitors must observe the latest Principle 20.04 on attending Advocates at

Court at **www.guide-on-line.lawsociety.org.uk**. This Principle replaces Principle 20.04 as it appeared in the print edition of *The Guide to the Professional Conduct of Solicitors 1999.*

2.12 APPROACH TO ADVOCACY

2.12.1 Solicitors are reminded of the need to comply with the Law Society's Code for Advocacy (Guide, Principle 21.02).

2.12.2 In any court hearing, solicitors should be extremely careful about their approach to other advocates and be even-handed in their approach to them and their clients. It is important that the whole of the case, and especially examination in court and cross-examination, is conducted in language which is understood by the child (if present in court), and that cross-examination is not aggressive and is limited to the pertinent issues. It is rare for it to be necessary for children to give evidence. Should they do so, solicitors must be alert to the natural anxiety of children about giving evidence.

2.12.3 Every effort should be made to keep the hearing strictly to the issues and as short as possible.

2.13 DISCLOSURE

2.13.1 From the outset, all solicitors for all parties should give careful consideration to the issue of disclosure.

2.13.2 The local authority should disclose all relevant information to the court and the other parties, including evidence favourable to the other parties.

2.13.3 The solicitors for the other parties should give early consideration as to whether the usual sources of information have been provided by the local authority, and any reasons for applying for further relevant disclosure of a particular document, or for access to a particular type of information (remembering that the children's guardian has access to the documentation prescribed under Children Act 1989, s.42).

2.13.4   Directions from the court should be sought on difficult issues of disclosure if necessary at the case management conference (Step 4 of the Protocol).

2.13.5   All solicitors must have knowledge of the implications in relation to disclosure of the common law duty of confidentiality, the Data Protection Act 1998 and the Human Rights Act 1998. A brief guide to data protection of personal information held by social services is attached at Appendix 5.

2.13.6   Reports should be read and anonymised as necessary before service and disclosure to other parties. Solicitors should always read documents before sending them out and consider whether to meet the client to discuss the contents of the document before giving him or her a copy. Any restrictions on the disclosure of information should be considered. If a solicitor is uncertain as to whether a particular document should be disclosed, particularly to a child client, directions from the court should be sought.

2.14   CONCURRENT CRIMINAL PROCEEDINGS

2.14.1   A solicitor should give very careful consideration to the issue of whether to act for a client in both sets of proceedings in accordance with professional rules. This can raise complex issues related to advising the client and in relation to requests for information on materials and reports seen by the solicitor in the other proceedings. It is generally advisable for a solicitor to decline to take instructions in the criminal proceedings if he or she is likely to be invited to act later in related Children Act proceedings.

2.14.2   Possible difficulties related to acting in both proceedings include:

(a)   receiving conflicting instructions from the client;

(b)   advising in relation to outcomes in both proceedings;

(c)   having constructive knowledge of an expert report adverse to the client's interests which may be required to be disclosed.

2.14.3 Solicitors should remember that the children's guardian is not automatically entitled to expert's reports filed in criminal proceedings.

2.14.4 Solicitors should be familiar with any procedures or arrangements in place in their area of practice for joint directions in respect of concurrent criminal and care proceedings. Solicitors should also consult the relevant Local Plan supporting the Protocol, which may be of assistance.

2.14.5 If two sets of solicitors are instructed, there should be careful liaison between them on the progress of the two sets of proceedings.

2.14.6 Solicitors should ask the relevant local authority and care centre whether any protocol or code of guidance for dealing with exchange of evidence and other information between the civil and criminal jurisdictions applies in the area, and seek to obtain a copy. The Code of Guidance for Disclosure of Police Information in Family Proceedings (see Appendix 6) will form the basis of an Association of Chief Police Officers (ACPO) pilot, and may be adopted nationally in due course. Local authority solicitors should know whether their local authority is party to a Protocol with the Crown Prosecution Service (CPS) and relevant police force on exchange of information in the investigation and prosecution of child abuse cases. A multi-agency working group led by the CPS has developed the protocol attached at Appendix 7.

2.15 COURT SECURITY

2.15.1 Solicitors should bring court safety issues to the attention of the court and other parties as early as possible in the proceedings. Any safety issues within the confines of the court building should be discussed with the court staff in advance.

2.15.2 Solicitors should consider the use of available video links for the giving of evidence, if appropriate.

2.16   LEAVING CARE

2.16.1   Solicitors should have knowledge of the Children (Leaving Care) Act 2000 which, *inter alia*, amends Children Act 1989, s.19 and ss.22–24 and the accompanying guidance.

PART 3

Local authority solicitors

3.1 INTRODUCTION

3.1.1 This part of the good practice guidance takes into account the guidance published by the Child Care Law Joint Liaison Group (Association of Council Secretaries and Solicitors in Local Government), 'Arrangements for Handling Child Care Cases' (revised September 2000), available in the family law specialism at **www.lawsociety.org.uk**. The Child Care Law Joint Liaison Group will be re-issuing their 'Arrangements' document so that it does not overlap with the guidance set out in this document. However, it will set out important guidance on other issues relevant to local authority solicitors, and Children Panel solicitors in private practice handling child care cases on behalf of a local authority legal department, with which those practitioners should be familiar.

3.1.2 The primary role of solicitors acting for local authorities is as follows:

(a)   to ensure the proper conduct of cases;

(b)   to ensure scrutiny of the local authority's case;

(c)   to safeguard the integrity of the local authority before the court: for example, to ensure through appropriate preparation and presentation that all relevant information is before the court and other parties;

(d)   to assist the court in its investigation and undertake all necessary steps to arrive at an appropriate result in the paramount interests of the welfare of the child.

3.1.3   No solicitor should represent a local authority in opposed child care without an up-to-date working knowledge of child care law, appropriate training in those areas not covered by experience in practice, and recent significant practical experience of conducting child care proceedings. It is desirable for all local authority child care lawyers to seek accreditation to the Law Society's Children Panel.

3.1.4   Local authority solicitors should be aware of the role and responsibility of their local Area Child Protection Committee. Solicitors should be aware of the different services and professional groups cooperating to safeguard the welfare of children. They should also be aware of any protocol and procedures between these agencies and the social services department that exist in order to enhance working together to safeguard children and to improve the quality of child protection work. Local authority solicitors should have regard to the importance of encouraging inter-departmental cooperation between the social services, education and housing departments.

3.2   RELATIONSHIP AND COMMUNICATION WITH CLIENT

3.2.1   The local authority solicitor's 'client' is the local authority, but the day-to-day working relationship is with the Director of Social Services, acting through managers and social workers. The Director will give legal advice on requests made by the social services department to start proceedings in relation to children. Solicitors should be familiar with the local authority's decision-making procedure on taking legal proceedings. In this connection, solicitors should be aware of the following:

(a)   Local authority solicitors have a duty as officers of the court to ensure that cases are dealt with appropriately, and this role transcends their duty to the client department. Coupled with the fact that the local authority solicitor's client is the local authority itself, many authorities will have in place a protocol or other agreement between the legal department and social services department, to regulate their working relationship and to deal with any disputes that might arise in the conduct of case work.

(b)   Connected to (a) above is the role of the local authority Monitoring Officer. Every local authority has to appoint a monitoring officer under the Local Government and Housing Act 1989, s.5. The role of the Monitoring Officer is to ensure that the authority acts at all times within the law and observes due process. The Monitoring Officer has statutory powers that can be exercised if he or she considers any proposed action of the authority to be unlawful.

3.2.2   The client should be advised that if contacted by solicitors for other parties during proceedings, those solicitors should be referred to the legal department for consent to deal with the client direct.

3.2.3   Special care should be taken when a decision is required on commencing proceedings in respect of a child. Decisions about the welfare and protection of a child should be taken within the social services department, which is where the necessary expertise to evaluate risk is to be found. Solicitors should not take decisions on matters within the province of the social services department.

3.2.4   Local authority solicitors should give advice to their clients about the legal strengths, weaknesses and complexities of their case before proceedings are commenced.

3.2.5   The local authority solicitor should be prepared to give advice on:

(a)   whether, in the circumstances of the case, and having regard to the s.1(3) checklist (the welfare checklist), the court is likely to be satisfied, first, that the s.31(2) criteria are satisfied (threshold for significant harm), and second, that there is a need for an order under s.1(5) ('no order' principle);

(b)   the implications of another party to the proceedings opposing the application and applying for a s.8 order instead;

(c)   whether transfer to another court will be appropriate and representations about this should be made at the First Hearing under the Protocol;

(d)   whether the evidence in the case satisfies the grounds for an interim care order, having regard to the paramountcy principle, the welfare checklist and the 'no order' principle, and the desired length of any initial interim order;

(e)   the initial social work statement and other local authority documents to be filed and served, and the procedural requirements under Step 1 of the Protocol;

(f)   the case management issues and directions likely to be considered at the First Hearing or the Allocation Hearing in accordance with the Protocol;

(g)   the alternative disposals available to the court as an appropriate alternative to a care order, for example, a residence order linked with a supervision order.

3.2.6   The steps involved in deciding whether or not a child should be made subject to care proceedings will inevitably be a complex process, requiring in-depth and regular consultation and discussion between lawyer and social worker. Their respective roles are significantly different, but when it comes to making a decision, there will be similar factors for both to consider, albeit from different perspectives.

3.2.7   Local authority solicitors should create and maintain a professional relationship with the local authority and its social services department, which will preserve fully their independent judgement.

3.3   BEFORE ISSUE OF PROCEEDINGS

3.3.1   It should be seen as in the local authority's interests for parents to have legal advice and representation from as early a stage as possible. Local authority solicitors have a role in reminding their social worker clients to be alert as to whether the family members have access to legal advice and of the role of their legal representatives. They should be advised to give information to family members on how to access legal advice, including the list of local Children Panel Children and Adult Party representatives (see Appendix 3).

3.3.2 Social services should be encouraged to request early legal planning meetings with legal departments. Where the social services department is making a request to take proceedings, a legal planning meeting should be held, as a matter of urgency if necessary, in order to advise the social worker client on the case and to prepare them for the commencement of the proceedings. The Victoria Climbie Inquiry Report recommended that 'no emergency action should be taken by a local authority on a case concerning an allegation of deliberate harm to a child without first obtaining legal advice' (recommendation 36). The following should be considered with the client:

(a)   the application;

(b)   whether the client has fully reviewed the history of the case: that is, whether they have reviewed all the files;

(c)   whether there is a complete set of all previous assessments of the family, minutes of statutory reviews and child protection conferences;

(d)   the evidential weight of the support work and assessments carried out to date, and whether further assessments will be required;

(e)   whether written information has been obtained from all other involved agencies and third parties on whom the local authority wishes to rely;

(f)   whether a running chronology has been kept at the top of the social work file and the updating of the running chronology as necessary;

(g)   the interim care plan and whether the plan takes into account the outcome of the child protection conferences and plans;

(h)   whether there is complete information on the wider family and friendship networks for the purposes of permanency planning.

3.3.3 From the outset, local authority solicitors should be alert to the need both to ensure information about family and friendship networks is available for the purposes of planning interim care for the child while the proceedings are pending, as expected by the Protocol, and to parallel (or twin-track) plan throughout in appropriate cases in order to avoid delay.

3.3.4 Reasonable but robust efforts should be made at an early stage to locate both parents, notably non-resident parents, and to identify members of the extended family. The primary carer's interpretation as to who is significant to the child should not necessarily be relied upon.

3.4 THE CONDUCT OF CASES

3.4.1 Local authority solicitors should seek to provide clarity of case for the court and other parties.

3.4.2 Bearing in mind that proceedings affect the continuing relationship with the family, solicitors should seek to achieve a constructive solution to the child's best interests, without prejudicing the child's interests.

3.4.3 Local authority solicitors should ensure that the social workers and other professionals involved with the child and the family are informed of their involvement and all other relevant details.

3.4.4 The solicitor is responsible for ensuring the integrity of the local authority's case before the court. Their duty is to consider all the evidence and to make the local authority's case, submitting balanced evidence that is true to the facts, fair and complete, full and frank. All relevant information should be shared with the court and other parties, including evidence favourable to the other parties.

3.4.5 All local authority solicitors should adhere to the guidance set out in Chapter 4, 'The local authority legal adviser', in the handbook *Reporting to Court under the Children Act* by Plotnikoff and Woolfson (Department of Health, 1996).

3.4.6 They should ensure that full cooperation is given to the children's guardian in the performance of his or her duties. Such cooperation should include advising social services to provide access to the appropriate case files in accordance with Children Act 1989, s.42.

3.4.7 The client will know the background information in relation to the case and the children's guardian will have access to the case files. It should not be assumed that the parents' solicitors will have copies of all papers sent to the parents. It is good practice to provide them, at the earliest opportunity, with copies of the papers relating to the child protection process, which the parents should have, such as case conference minutes.

3.4.8 The client should be kept informed throughout the case. The solicitor with responsibility for the case should keep social workers, and other professionals as appropriate, informed of the state and stage of the proceedings, and the reasons for and implications of any changes in plan or delays.

3.4.9 Social workers, particularly the less experienced, are likely to need an explanation of the roles of those involved in the case, for example the children's guardian and the judge.

3.4.10 The solicitor with responsibility for the case should also ensure that social workers understand what will be expected of them when they attend court. They should be reminded to bring the relevant files with them to meetings and hearings.

3.4.11 All correspondence in child care cases should be given the appropriate priority and copies sent to the social workers and/or others as necessary.

3.5   CARE PLANS DURING THE COURSE OF PROCEEDINGS

3.5.1 Local authority solicitors must be familiar with Appendix F of the Protocol, the 'Social Services Assessment and Care Planning Aide-Memoire' at **www.courtservice.gov.uk/using_ courts/protocol/index.htm**. All parties should recognise that a successful outcome for the child may require flexibility. Local authority solicitors should ensure that the care plan before the court accurately reflects the situation of the child and any significant change in circumstances. Where proceedings are before the court, except in cases of emergency, the local authority solicitor should advise the client that there should be no significant change in the child's circumstances without prior consultation with the children's guardian and without taking into account the wishes and feelings of the parents and any other relevant person.

3.5.2 Local authority solicitors should bring to the attention of the court any significant changes to the final care plan in time for the pre-hearing review, again having advised the client as in para. 3.5.1.

3.5.3 Regard should be had to the contents of and changes in other local authority plans which may overlap with the care plan, for example pathway plans for looked after children, and education plans.

3.6 EXPERTS

3.6.1 The inappropriate or unnecessary use of experts in care proceedings can often lead to delay for the child and expense for the local authority. It is essential that all local authority lawyers are aware of the local authority's policy for the instruction and funding of experts. The need for and reasons to instruct an expert should be discussed with the social worker client.

3.7 THE USE OF COUNSEL

3.7.1 Solicitors should be aware of the legal department's general policy with regard to the instruction of counsel.

3.8 AFTER CONCLUSION OF PROCEEDINGS

3.8.1 Social workers should be reminded of the significance and importance of the main provisions of the final care plan approved by the court, and to keep a copy of that plan in its entirety on the social services file, to form the basis for future care planning.

3.8.2 Social workers should be advised that if any significant departure from the final care plan is planned at any stage, it should be discussed as far as possible in a timely manner with the child, the child's parents and/or any other person with parental responsibility, and legal advice sought in order that the local authority solicitor can begin advising and planning as appropriate.

3.8.3 Consideration should be given to the need to commence a Criminal Injuries Compensation Authority (CICA) action where the child is made the subject of a care order.

PART 4

Solicitors instructed by children or children's guardians

4.1 INTRODUCTION

4.1.1 Solicitors instructed by children's guardians or directly by children in public law proceedings should be children representatives of the Law Society's Children Panel.

4.1.2 A children's guardian appointed in public law cases has a duty to advise the court what is in the child's best interests from their professional point of view, and has a duty to communicate the child's wishes to the court. The children's guardian will appoint a solicitor whose client is the child.

4.1.3 The solicitor takes instructions from the children's guardian when the child is not sufficiently mature to instruct directly, or when the child is sufficiently mature and his or her instructions do not conflict with the children's guardian's views. The mature child who is in conflict with the children's guardian will give instructions directly to his or her solicitor, and the child's instructions must be followed (as with any other client), even if contrary to the client's interests as perceived by the solicitor.

4.1.4 In circumstances when a solicitor is appointed for a child who is not competent to give instructions, and no children's guardian has been appointed, it is the solicitor's professional duty to act in the child's best interests (see the 'Notice to Children Panel Members' issued by the Law Society in October 2003, Appendix 8).

4.1.5 It is important to distinguish between a situation in which the solicitor is taking instructions from the children's guardian (in which case this guidance should be read in conjunction with Appendix 10) and one in which the solicitor is taking instructions directly from the child. The distinction should be borne in mind when following this guidance on the relationship between solicitor and child. Solicitors acting for or contacted by children, when there is or may be a conflict between the children's guardian and the competent child, should be familiar with the SFLA's *Guide to Good Practice for Solicitors Acting for Children* (sixth edition, 2002), obtainable from SFLA, taken into account in this Part. The SFLA regularly updates this guide. Solicitors are encouraged to ensure that they have obtained the most recent version from SFLA (see contact details in Appendix 11).

4.2 ROLE OF SOLICITOR WHERE NO CHILDREN'S GUARDIAN IS ALLOCATED

4.2.1   Solicitors should read and observe the 'Notice to Children Panel Members', issued by the Law Society in October 2003, at Appendix 8.

4.2.2   Solicitors will be appointed by the court in accordance with the 'Statement of Good Practice in the Appointment of Solicitors for Children where it Falls to the Court to do so in Specified Proceedings', applicable from 8 December 2003 and accompanying the Protocol. This is available at **www.lawsociety.org.uk** in the family specialism section. Solicitors should receive from the court copies of the papers, further to Step 1 of the Protocol. Solicitors should contact the local authority's legal department for further papers available.

4.2.3   Pending the allocation of a children's guardian, solicitors should keep the relevant CAFCASS office informed of prioritisation needs and the court timetable so that these can be taken into account when allocating a children's guardian. It is good practice to seek to contact CAFCASS after the First Hearing and to respond promptly to requests for information from CAFCASS.

4.2.4   Solicitors should consider applying to the court for leave to instruct an independent social worker who may be paid as a disbursement under the child's certificate. See the LSC's guidance in *Focus 40* (December 2002).

4.2.5   A variety of materials are available to assist children and young people who are the subject of care proceedings to understand the court process and the different roles of the professionals involved. Solicitors may wish to distribute to children the *Power Pack,* published in two versions by the NSPCC in conjunction with CAFCASS, one for older and one for younger children, if there is to be delay in the allocation of a children's guardian. The *Power Pack* is designed to assist children and young people to understand the court process and the different roles of the professionals. It is worth asking local courts and CAFCASS regional offices if they have available stocks. Otherwise the packs can be downloaded or ordered at a postage and packing charge from **www.nspcc.org.uk/inform** (click on publications).

4.3   WORKING RELATIONSHIPS WITH CHILDREN'S GUARDIANS

4.3.1   Solicitors should read and observe the 'Guidance on the Working Relationship between Children Panel Solicitors and Children's Guardians' at Appendix 10. This replaces the 'Protocol for the Working Relationship between Children Panel Solicitors and Guardians *ad litem*', issued in March 2000.

4.3.2   Solicitors should advise children's guardians to be, and be seen as, even-handed towards the parties throughout. Children's guardians should be encouraged only to take a particular position at an early stage in the case when it is necessary to meet the needs of the child, for example in relation to the issue of immediate removal. Those representing the child should be alert to the impact on the parents of taking more than a preliminary view on the basis of limited, partial evidence. The independence of the children's guardian and child's solicitor can often be used to reduce conflict and broker agreements throughout, and therefore must not be compromised.

4.3.3   Solicitors have a duty to the court not to mislead. Whilst it is important for the solicitor as advocate to represent the child's case on the instructions of the children's guardian or the child, it is also part of that solicitor's duty to ensure that any relevant but unclear issue is rigorously explored and evidence clarified. This may include the need to breach solicitor–client confidentiality in relation to a child, whatever the possible implications for the position of the children's guardian.

4.3.4 There is a lack of clarity as to the role of the children's guardian at causation hearings. This issue requires careful consideration. The child's solicitor should consider raising at directions at an early stage the issue of planning for the causation hearing, including the role (if any) of the children's guardian and attendance of the children's guardian at that hearing. If the court decides that the children's guardian's attendance is not required, the child's solicitor must still attend and, whenever possible, make arrangements with the children's guardian for the taking of instructions, if necessary.

4.4 SEEING THE CHILD

4.4.1 As a general principle, the solicitor should always meet the child, whether taking instructions from the children's guardian or directly from the child. Consideration should be given to the most appropriate setting and style for such meetings. The length and venue of interviews should be appropriate to the child's needs and the interview should be and taken at the child's pace. In cases involving young children, or those under profound disability, solicitors should not assume that they do not have to see their clients. Once seen, the child will continue to be valued as an individual client throughout the proceedings. Clearly the number of visits will depend on the level of the child's understanding of his or her current situation. The solicitor should not assume that it will be sufficient to see the child only once.

4.4.2 When making arrangements to see the child, it is advisable to bear in mind the child's age and familiarity with meetings. Consultation with the child's social worker and the children's guardian may assist, and the children's guardian may introduce the solicitor to the child. A child or young person who has had a long history of being looked after may be experienced in attending meetings. For such a young person, a meeting in the office may not present such difficulties as may be faced by a less experienced child of any age. Consideration should be given as to whether, for example, the child's home, foster home or school will provide a sensitive and safe environment to meet the child.

Solicitors should be sensitive as to whether a child would want any interview to take place at school or whether it is appropriate for a child to be removed for an interview during school hours.

4.4.3 Solicitors should be alert to issues of safety for both the solicitor and the child, and the possible vulnerability of the child. It may be necessary for solicitors to consider whether to see a child alone or not. Again, consultation with the child's social worker and children's guardian may assist. Solicitors should record where they see the child and why.

4.4.4 Solicitors should be alert to confidentiality issues for both the parents and the child when seeing the child at home.

4.4.5 It is important when taking instructions from a child or young person that sufficient time is allowed to ensure instructions can be given in a relaxed and unhurried manner. This is particularly important at court hearings.

4.5 ASSESSING UNDERSTANDING/COMPETENCE TO GIVE INSTRUCTIONS

4.5.1 From the outset, and throughout the case, the solicitor should be alert to the child's level of understanding and capacity to give instructions about the case.

4.5.2 In practice, a decision on the child's capacity and ability to give instructions will need to be made where a conflict arises or is likely to arise between the child and the children's guardian.

4.5.3 This can be assessed on the basis of the child's age and ability to understand the nature of the proceedings and to have an appreciation of the possible consequences of the applications before the court, both in the long and short term.

Philip King and Ian Young in *The Child as Client* (Family Law, 1992) provide a useful checklist:

'To be competent, the child should understand the following (which should not be regarded as exhaustive):

- the solicitor's role
- the nature of the proceedings in respect of which the child is subject

- the reasons for the proceedings
- what takes place at court
- what other professionals think is best for the child
- what the child's parents and other parties to proceedings think is best for the child
- in care proceedings, the analysis of the Children's Guardian and the threshold criteria which must be proved.'

4.5.4 A solicitor alert to a potential or clear conflict should notify the children's guardian of the child's wishes and feelings with the child's consent, and discuss with him or her the issue of separate representation for the child and the children's guardian.

4.5.5 A child with capacity to give instructions with a contrary view to the children's guardian may not wish to give their own instructions, however. In such a case, the solicitor should make clear to both the child and the children's guardian that the child has the right not to advance a case, and advise the children's guardian to explain to the child and the other parties (having informed the child of their intention of doing so) that the child's view is contrary to the children's guardian's instructions.

4.5.6 In the first instance, it is the duty of the solicitor, not that of the children's guardian, to assess a child's understanding, although advice can be sought from the children's guardian. If there is conflict on the issue of competence the court will make the final judgement, and it may be necessary to produce evidence where the court is minded to make a different judgement to the solicitor. It is important for the child to understand that the solicitor's judgement as to his or her capacity may be overruled by the court. The solicitor should discuss with the children's guardian who should inform the child of any court decision, as appropriate.

4.5.7 Where in a solicitor's judgement there is a conflict between the child and the children's guardian, and the child has capacity to give instructions, the solicitor should formally notify the children's guardian that he or she can no longer be represented by the solicitor, and all parties and the court should be notified of the solicitor's position. Instructions should be taken directly from the child unless, and until, the court rules otherwise. In these circumstances it is for the children's guardian to make an application for leave for separate legal representation, if he or she requires it.

4.5.8 If the solicitor is in doubt as to the child's capacity to give instructions, and what the child says is in conflict with the children's guardian, the solicitor should seek the advice of one of the other professionals involved in the case, such as a child psychiatrist, social worker or teacher, or should approach an independent expert (for example, a child psychiatrist/psychologist). When making these consultations solicitors should remain sensitive to the duty of confidentiality to the child. Ultimately, if the solicitor cannot decide on the child's level of understanding, an application can be made to the court.

4.5.9 As the proceedings progress, the solicitor will need to explain to the child giving direct instructions, and the child will need to understand, such factors as what parents and other parties want for the child, and what the children's guardian and other experts recommend for the child.

4.5.10 If the child loses capacity to give instructions, the court should be informed and where instructions are withdrawn by the child, the court must be informed. If it appears that the child's decision-making ability has become impaired, the solicitor should reassess the child's capacity and consult with the children's guardian, or other professionals involved, being careful not to breach the child's confidentiality or prejudice the child's case. If need be, an application may be made to the court on notice for the leave to instruct a solicitor directly to be rescinded, or for other suitable directions.

4.5.11 Where a child approaches a solicitor direct and where no proceedings are issued or pending, the solicitor is likely to wish to meet the child to establish a preliminary view as to the child's understanding or maturity. Even if not sufficiently competent to give instructions for the purposes of proceedings, the solicitor may judge the child as sufficiently mature and competent to receive independent advice, probably under Legal Help. It should be established whether the child's parents, and/or the local authority in the case of a looked after child, know that the child is seeking advice, and the child should be encouraged to agree that they be notified of the same. If the child insists that they not be notified, the solicitor's duty of confidentiality must be observed subject to an exception applying (see the Guide, Principle 16.02, Note 4).

4.6 RELATIONSHIP AND COMMUNICATION WITH CHILD

4.6.1 The solicitor should be alert to the particular needs of the individual child, for example for interpreters and translations, whether taking instructions from the children's guardian or directly from the child. It is not the role of the solicitor to act as interpreter between the child and other professionals involved in the case, even if able to speak the child's first language.

4.6.2 Solicitors should not take direct instructions from a child when they do not speak the language of the child and no interpreter is available.

4.6.3 When receiving instructions directly from the child, the solicitor should keep the child informed in an appropriate manner, as with any other client. The solicitor should carefully consider whether to write to the child on particular matters or perhaps at all, and the address letters should be sent to. The solicitor should record in writing the reasons for decisions.

4.6.4 When solicitors receive instructions from a children's guardian, the extent of their communication with the child and provision of information to the child about the case will be a matter of judgement to be considered with the children's guardian in each case. In any event, solicitors should also consider writing to children before final hearings.

4.6.5 Whoever gives the instructions, the child is always a party to the proceedings and the solicitor's client. It is therefore important for the child to have continuing contact with their solicitor by visits and/or letters and for the solicitor to build a relationship with the child, although the frequency of contact will depend on the circumstances of the case and the child. The solicitor should consider the importance for the child of a written record about the proceedings for the future.

4.7 CONFIDENTIALITY

4.7.1 When acting for any child, the duty of confidentiality exists as it does for the adult client. This duty always exists save in the exceptional circumstances summarised below.

4.7.2 The child client should be made aware of the duty of confidentiality and when and how the solicitor's duty of confidentiality may be breached in appropriate circumstances. This should also be explained, if possible, to any younger, less mature child in an appropriate way and according to his or her level of understanding, after consultation with the children's guardian.

4.7.3 Where a children's guardian is appointed, it is important for solicitors to ensure that the mature child consents to information being given to the children's guardian (who is not a client). Even if no potential conflict exists, consent should still be obtained.

4.7.4 What any child tells his or her solicitor is subject to the solicitor's duty of confidentiality. The child should be advised, as appropriate (in practice this is likely to apply to the mature child), that if he or she wants a discussion to be confidential it should be with his or her solicitor, subject to the exceptions below applying. What the child tells the children's guardian is not confidential. However, if, for example, the child will only tell the solicitor with whom he or she wants to live, and asks for this not to be disclosed, the solicitor should explain to the child that the child's views will not be known if he or she insists on confidentiality.

4.7.5 If the child's solicitor finds himself or herself to be in conflict with the children's guardian, the duty of confidentiality is owed to the client (the child). No information should be disclosed to the children's guardian, or any other person without the child's consent, unless an exception to the solicitor's duty of confidentiality applies.

4.7.6 It may be necessary to breach confidentiality in relation to a child against the child client's wishes:

(a) Where the child reveals information which indicates continuing sexual or other physical abuse, but refuses to allow disclosure of such information, the solicitor must consider whether the threat to the child's life or health, both mental and physical, is sufficiently serious to justify a breach of the duty of confidentiality (Guide, Principle 16.02, Note 4).

(b) There is a duty to disclose experts' reports obtained in the course of proceedings even if adverse (Guide, Principle 16.02, Note 5).

(c) In relation to disclosure of adverse material not obtained within the course of proceedings, in exceptional cases to do otherwise would breach the solicitor's duty not to mislead the court (Guide, Principle 16.02, Note 5).

(d) Where the solicitor is summoned as a witness or subpoenaed, the court may direct the solicitor to disclose documentation or divulge information.

4.7.7 However, solicitors should always bear in mind that they owe a duty of confidentiality to their clients and may have to justify any breach of that duty to their professional body. It is always advisable to seek advice from Professional Ethics on 0870 606 2577, mentors, other members of the profession, partners in the firm and/or professional insurers.

4.8   CONFLICTS OF INTEREST BETWEEN CHILDREN

4.8.1 Where the solicitor is representing more than one child in the proceedings, he/she must be aware of the possibility of a conflict arising not only between a child and the children's guardian, but also between the children. It will be necessary to determine how many of the children are of sufficient understanding to instruct the solicitor direct.

4.8.2 If there is a conflict, either between two or more mature children, or between a mature child and the children's guardian in relation to other children, solicitors must consider whether they can continue to act for any of the children involved in the light of information received at the time. It is impossible for an advocate both to support the care plan and at the same time challenge that plan on behalf of one dissenting child. Where solicitors take the view that they must cease acting for all or some of the children, they should inform the children, the children's guardian and the court of the position, so that separate representation can be arranged. Solicitors must decide which children (if any) they will continue to represent and should help the mature children seek alternative representation.

4.8.3 In such situations, consultation with the children's guardian is essential and guidance from the court by way of directions may have to be sought. Whatever the decision, solicitors must be mindful of the existing and continuing duty of confidentiality to the child.

4.8.4 When a solicitor is acting for several children and the extent of access to the evidence afforded varies, solicitors should warn children to whom documents are disclosed, that such documents are strictly confidential and should not be shown to those who are not entitled to see them.

4.9   THE CONDUCT OF CASES

4.9.1 Solicitors representing a child should ensure that all the other professionals involved are informed of their involvement and all other relevant details.

4.9.2 Care and caution should be taken when acting on a child's direct instructions in terms of testing and evaluating the parents' contribution to significant harm. The solicitor should clarify the facts, bring inaccuracies to the court's attention and set out the child's story, without making judgements about the parents. However, the child may specifically wish for his or her perception of the parents' contribution to significant harm, for example, in cases of physical and sexual abuse, to be expressed to the court.

4.9.3 A solicitor should ensure a child giving direct instructions as client has sufficient information to be able to make informed decisions. However, solicitors should be aware that the client may feel under pressure to agree to a course of action in a wish to please and later regret such a decision. It is important to proceed at the child's pace and allow the child to change course or ultimately withdraw. It is easy for solicitors effectively to take over a case and solicitors should be sensitive to this risk. The obligation to take instructions and give robust advice is the same as for an adult client, save that the advice must always be given in terms that the child can understand. The child must be helped to understand that although the court will know of the child's wishes, it will make its decision based on that which is perceived to be in the child's interests.

4.9.4 Any statement by the child must represent the child's evidence as to fact, the child's views on the issues and their wishes, and insofar as is possible, to be in the child's own words. The statement should indicate that the child understands it is his or her duty to speak the truth and is a declaration as required by the Family Proceedings Rules (FPR) 1991, rule 4.17. If a child makes a statement then he or she can be cross-examined on it; the solicitor should consider whether this is the best way to present the evidence.

4.10 EXPERTS

4.10.1 Solicitors must be aware of the need to advise any child client of sufficient understanding to make an informed decision of his or her statutory right to refuse consent to medical or psychiatric assessment or treatment. The child should be warned that in certain circumstances, the court may override his or her decision.

4.10.2 In proceedings under the Children Act 1989, solicitors are under a duty to disclose expert reports commissioned in the course of proceedings. Before instructing an expert, the child giving instructions should be warned like any other client of the risks involved in seeking reports which may contain adverse information or opinion (see the Guide, Principle 16.02, Note 5). The child client needs to be warned that a solicitor is an officer of the court, and an advocate cannot mislead the court by act or omission, therefore such documents may have to be disclosed even if adverse. Where the children's guardian has given the instructions, the solicitor should discuss this with him or her.

4.10.3 Careful consideration should be given by the solicitor before discussing with the child the selection of the expert and the letter of instruction. The child or the children's guardian should be reminded that any expert instructed should be unbiased.

4.10.4 Where chairing an experts' meeting, the child's solicitor must be mindful of the issues and the need for an unpartisan view.

4.11   CHILD'S ACCESS TO DOCUMENTS

4.11.1 The solicitor is generally under a duty to allow all clients, including child clients, unfettered access to any relevant documentary evidence which the solicitor holds, save where such evidence would adversely affect the client's physical or mental condition (see the Guide, Principle 16.06). Generally, as a matter of good practice, there may be exceptional cases such as serious child sexual abuse when the nature of the document is such that it would be inappropriate for clients to be sent a copy of the document. When representing a child, solicitors should be particularly careful about showing documents to their client. Where solicitors are instructed by a children's guardian, they should discuss sending any documentation, and requests for documentation made by the child, with the children's guardian. If in any doubt as to whether a document should be disclosed to a child giving direct instructions, the solicitor should seek the opinion of the children's guardian or another professional involved in the case. Speaking to a senior colleague or another Children Panel solicitor may also be of help. Ultimately, directions can be sought from the court as to non-disclosure.

4.11.2 Care should be exercised before copies of documents are given to child clients to keep. It is likely to be inappropriate to send a child client copies of documentation through the post. It is likely to be more appropriate to visit the child and talk them through the documentation.

4.11.3 Solicitors acting for a child should be aware that if a local authority holds personal information about their client, the child has a right of access to that information unless an exception applies. There are similar regulations that give a right of access to education and health records.

4.12   IN COURT

4.12.1   The solicitor should consider the options for the child's attendance at court, whether taking instructions from the children's
guardian or directly from the child, and discuss matters with the
children's guardian or the child. The solicitor should consider
whether the child might:

(a)   never go to the court;

(b)   visit the court before a substantive hearing as part of
understanding what is happening, whether or not the
child will come to the hearing;

(c)   attend the hearing but not give evidence and either sit in
or outside the hearing;

(d)   attend the hearing for the purposes of giving evidence.

4.12.2   There is currently much discussion on creative ways to involve
children in the decision-making process and to ensure that their
voice is heard. Solicitors should keep themselves informed of
practice developments in this area.

4.12.3   The child can attend court hearings if he or she wishes to do so,
but this should be discussed with the child who should be
warned that he or she may be excluded by the court. It may be
helpful to discuss the issue of the child's attendance at court
with the other professionals involved in the case. The solicitor
should be sensitive to the fact the child may not wish to be in
close physical proximity to certain parties in and outside the
court.

4.12.4   If the child attends the hearing, the solicitor should warn the
child that they may hear evidence which may be upsetting and
the solicitor should be sensitive to the child's emotional state
throughout the hearing.

4.12.5   The solicitor should offer to show the child the court room and
make sure that there are arrangements for the child if the child
asks to leave the hearing. Suitable arrangements should be
made for someone to sit with the child.

4.12.6   It is generally highly unusual for the child to meet the magistrates or judge either before or after the court makes its decision,

but this may depend on local practice. In some cases the judge or magistrates may suggest a private meeting. The solicitor should ensure that the child is comfortable with the proposals and whoever accompanies the child, and be clear about the basis on which any meeting takes place.

4.12.7 Solicitors should take whatever steps they can, as appropriate, to facilitate a meeting where a child expresses a wish to meet the judge or magistrates, but should liaise with the children's guardian, be careful not to raise the child's expectations and be clear about the basis on which any meeting takes place.

4.12.8 Before any meeting, the child should be made aware that the conversation will not be confidential.

4.12.9 The solicitor may wish to consider with the child whether the child would like to write a letter to the judge or magistrates, which could be read in court.

4.13   THE CHILD AS WITNESS

4.13.1 The child's evidence may be given if the court considers that the child understands the duty to speak the truth and that he or she has sufficient understanding to justify the giving of evidence (Children Act 1989, ss.96(1) and (2)).

4.13.2 Whether or not a mature child should give evidence in court is a matter which will have to be considered carefully by the solicitor with the child, after full discussions with the children's guardian where they are giving instructions. The child's evidence can be given by a third party relying on the rule that hearsay evidence is admissible in family proceedings under the Children (Admissibility of Hearsay Evidence) Order 1993. However, where the child's evidence is particularly relevant to the issues in the case, the fact that hearsay evidence is not as cogent as real evidence will need to be borne in mind when considering with the child whether he or she will give evidence.

4.13.3 In any consideration of whether or not the child should give evidence, the solicitor should ensure that it is the child who decides. If the child files a statement, the child should be warned he or she may have to give evidence and be cross-examined.

Solicitors should bear in mind that there will be limited instances where, if the evidence is relevant and the child wants to give evidence, it may be therapeutic or enabling for the child to have the opportunity to give evidence.

4.13.4 The solicitor should consider and advise upon the likelihood of the child giving evidence before the hearing. The child is likely to be worried about speaking in court and needs to know if this is likely. In relation to the substantive evidence to be given by a child, it is important not to coach the child, but it would be acceptable to give him or her an idea of the kind of questions which will be asked. The child should know that it is all right to say that he or she cannot remember (if this is the case) or does not understand the question. Generally the more information the child can be given about what is likely to happen, the easier it will be for the child to give evidence in a relaxed manner, with the minimum of trauma. Opening evidence in chief should be by way of gentle questions dealing with non-contentious issues, to enable the child to relax.

4.13.5 If the child is to give evidence, he or she should be reassured about the privacy of the proceedings but told of the other people who will be in the court room. This includes court staff, particularly ushers who may be wearing black gowns and in respect of whom the child may have wholly unrealistic ideas. The solicitor should arrange a visit to the court on a day before the hearing takes place. Provided the courtroom is not in use, ushers and staff are always willing to facilitate such visits. It is the solicitor's duty to check what arrangements are made for the child to give evidence (for example, behind a screen) if it is appropriate in the circumstances of the case. The solicitor may need to seek directions at an early stage in the proceedings. The solicitor should establish with other advocates whether or not they anticipate extensive cross-examination, and encourage them to consider the child's natural anxiety about giving evidence and to limit their cross-examination to the pertinent issues.

4.13.6 Solicitors should also do all they can to minimise the time the child has to wait outside the court, as this naturally increases the child's anxiety. Arrangements should be made to use the care room or children's suite at the court (if the court is so equipped).

4.14   AFTER CONCLUSION OF PROCEEDINGS

4.14.1   Solicitors should consider with the children's guardian, when the children's guardian is giving instructions, the best way of advising the child of the outcome. In practice the guidance in paragraphs 4.14.2 and 4.14.3 will be most relevant where the solicitor has taken instructions direct from the child, but should be borne in mind for any child client.

4.14.2   The solicitor should ensure that he or she remains accessible to the child and is sympathetic yet professional. Over-dependence by either the child or solicitor on the other should be discouraged. It should, however, be noted that some children may wish to keep in touch with their solicitor from time to time. Care should always be exercised in such a situation because the solicitor–client relationship has ended, and continued communication might compromise the solicitor's future representation of that child in any future or subsequent proceedings.

4.14.3   It is important that the solicitor prepares the child for the end of the relationship and begins telling the child, before the end of the case, that the solicitor's role will shortly be over.

4.14.4   When the solicitor's role is over, solicitors should ensure, through the children's guardian if more appropriate, that the child:

(a)   has access to information about the local authority's responsibilities to him or her;

(b)   is aware of the right to complain about matters concerning his or her welfare in care, if appropriate, and may make further applications to the court.

This should be done in person and confirmed by letter to which the child could refer at a later stage. It is important, however, not to undermine the child's relationship with his or her carers or the re-establishment of family relationships which may have been under pressure during the course of proceedings.

4.15 MATERIALS FOR USE WITH CHILD

4.15.1 During the course of proceedings, the solicitor should consider introducing the child to what is happening in the case
through other materials, in particular the *Power Pack* at
www.nspcc.org.uk/inform and the CAFCASS website at
www.cafcass.gov.uk. After the conclusion of proceedings, it may
be helpful to direct the child to other sources of information for
future reference. For those children subject to final or interim
care orders, the website run by the SFLA in conjunction with
NCH at **www.carelaw.org.uk** is recommended.

PART 5

Solicitors instructed by parents and other adult parties

5.1 INTRODUCTION

5.1.1 Much of this guidance will apply to both solicitors acting for parents and those acting for other adult parties. It is the role of such solicitors:

(a) to ensure the proper conduct of cases;

(b) to test the local authority and children's guardian's case on behalf of their client;

(c) to present their client's case to the court and all others involved in the case in an appropriate manner.

Clients should be advised that the court will be deciding the case in the child's best interests and therefore recommend a child-centred approach. Nevertheless, solicitors must follow their client's instructions and advocate their case in court, even if those instructions are not, in their view, in the client's best interests.

5.1.2 No solicitor should represent an adult party in child care proceedings unless competent to do so. Solicitors are reminded in particular of Principle 12.03 of the Guide and Part IV of the Law Society's Code for Advocacy. It is desirable for solicitors to seek accreditation to the Law Society's Children Panel.

5.2 CLIENTS UNDER A DISABILITY

5.2.1 Solicitors must bear in mind that they cannot be retained by clients incapable of giving instructions. A solicitor should not assume that a client under a legal disability is incapable of giving instructions.. Care should be taken when assessing the capacity of those under 18 or those, for example with learning disabilities, mental health problems, brain damage, or any combination of these characteristics.

5.2.2 A solicitor consulted by a client who cannot give instructions must identify a willing and suitable next friend or guardian *ad litem* to conduct any litigation (FPR 1991, rule 9.2). The Official Solicitor will act in the absence of anyone else willing and suitable (*Practice Note, Official Solicitor: Appointment of Family Proceedings* [2001] 2 FLR 155). A CAFCASS officer cannot fulfil a role on behalf of an adult party incapable of giving instructions.

5.2.3 If a solicitor is in any doubt about whether a client (or the other party) is a patient for the purposes of FPR 1991, rule 9.1 the Official Solicitor can provide a standard medical certificate to be completed by the person's medical attendant.

5.3 RELATIONSHIP AND COMMUNICATION WITH CLIENT

5.3.1 Regardless of whether or not there are proceedings, or if the child is already a looked after child, the client should be encouraged if possible to bring to the first meeting all documentation in their possession including child protection conference minutes and reports, or statutory review minutes.

5.3.2 Clients often do not realise the significance of documentation sent to them by social services departments and other agencies. Solicitors should advise clients to keep possession of all documentation received at any stage in relation to the children, whether they are looked after children or not. Solicitors should request copies of any documentation from the local authority legal department, which the clients should have but which are not immediately available.

5.3.3 It is reiterated that adult clients should be advised and encouraged to attend any family group conference and all child protection conferences. If the client is unclear about the concerns of the local authority and what he or she is expected to do to overcome them, the solicitor should write to the local authority asking for this to be confirmed in writing.

5.3.4   At the commencement of every case, solicitors should send clients a letter of retainer confirming their instructions, the extent of the retainer and any limits placed upon them by clients. They should ensure that the client verifies that the letter reflects accurately the instructions given, and understand the effects of the instructions and the limitations. The letter should normally be sent to the client following the first meeting.

5.3.5   At the end of the first meeting, or as soon as possible, solicitors should outline likely outcomes to the client in writing as far as this is practical on the information available. Advice should also be given about how the case is likely to proceed. It is important that clients are not given unrealistic expectations of what can be achieved nor unrealistic expectations of the time a matter may take to resolve. If the client is unable to read, arrangements should be made to provide this information in person.

5.3.6   If, at any time during the conduct of a case, the client decides to ignore advice given by a solicitor, or to act in a way that the solicitor considers to be unreasonable, unwise or detrimental to that client's interests, the solicitor must write to the client expressing these concerns and the consequences of the action proposed by the client, including in relation to public funding as appropriate. In practice, in light of the nature of the proceedings and the human rights implications of a parent or person with parental responsibility being unrepresented, the public funding consequences are only likely to be an issue where solicitors are without instructions. It is advisable to discuss all the circumstances with the LSC as withdrawal of public funding is a drastic step in care proceedings.

5.3.7   Solicitors are advised to check whether the client lives in multi-occupied premises, in order to consider whether it is appropriate to send any sensitive materials to the particular client's address or to ask that he or she come into the office to collect it. Materials involving for instance, child sex abuse, should not be released if there is a risk that they will be passed to the wrong people. There is a particular risk of this if the client is in prison.

5.3.8   Solicitors should be alert to the particular needs of individual clients, for example, for interpreters and translations. Where English is not the first language, solicitors should always consider whether an interpreter should be present throughout an interview. Solicitors should not act for a client when they do not speak the language of the client and no interpreter is available. Professional interpreters should be used wherever possible. Solicitors should be alert to the fact that interpreters found within the community are sometimes not independent.

5.3.9   Solicitors should allow sufficient time for the taking of instructions at every stage of the proceedings, particularly where clients are non-English speaking or have other communication difficulties. Clients may need to be taken through their own and other statements more than once.

5.3.10 Solicitors should seek to ensure that, as far as possible, the client is given the opportunity to fully participate in and be fully informed of what is happening in the case, even if there is a lack of documentation at any stage, in order to avoid the risk of the client feeling marginalised within the process.

5.3.11 It is important for solicitors to bear in mind and to emphasise to clients, throughout the case and as appropriate at the conclusion, the continuing nature of the relationship between the family and the local authority.

5.3.12 Where the client's instructions are to oppose the local authority's case, solicitors must ensure that they rigorously test the validity of that case and all the evidence, advising their clients appropriately on what evidence can be challenged and/or what will be difficult to successfully challenge. This will be the case when considering the threshold criteria or the evidence after assessments are completed, or in light of the proposed care plan. It also applies when an application for an emergency protection order is made, or on the first application for an interim care order. The draconian nature of a removal from home has recently been emphasised in decisions made under the Human Rights Act 1998 in *Re M (Care Proceedings: Judicial Review)* [2003] EWHC 850 (Admin); [2003] 2 FLR 171 and *Re B (Care: Interference with Family Life)* [2003] EWCA Civ 786. Solicitors are reminded that it is their responsibility to advise clients if, in their professional view, the court is likely to find that the threshold criteria are clearly established by the evidence. It is therefore important for the child, as well as the parents, that the parents work with the court and the other parties in particular in making any appropriate timely and constructive concession.

5.3.13   Where the threshold criteria are conceded or established, solicitors should be mindful when advising their clients of the importance of moving on in an open, constructive and cooperative way, for example, cooperating with any assessment designed to test their capacity to change.

5.3.14   Clients should generally be encouraged to be open and frank in their disclosure of information. They should be advised to 'reveal all' on the basis that matters will probably emerge in any event, and in order to enhance their chances of retaining care of or reunification with the child. Solicitors should also be mindful of the Children Act 1989, s.98 and associated case law on the relationship between criminal and care proceedings and advise their clients accordingly.

5.3.15   Advising clients in relation to the renewal of interim care orders can be a difficult issue where parents automatically or unreasonably instruct opposition to renewal. It should be made clear to clients that after the making of an interim care order which has been unsuccessfully opposed, there is a strong presumption towards retaining the status quo at further interim hearings. To mount a successful challenge the court will need to hear new information on a significant change of circumstances since the making of the last interim order: for example, new information on an unsuitable foster home.

5.3.16   Parents and other significant adults may have different views from those of the local authority, children's guardian and/or the court about what is in the child's best interests on disposal of the case. If this is the case, it is appropriate that full representations are made; however, solicitors must advise their clients that the court will approach disposal of the case from the viewpoint of what is best for the child, and that this can override views and wishes of the client and/or the child.

5.3.17   Solicitors should use their best efforts to dissuade clients from making wholly unmeritorious applications totally unsupported by the evidence; or which may be clearly motivated by intentions other than consideration for the children's welfare; and from opposing applications where the evidence is overwhelmingly not in their favour. Costs consequences should also be appropriately explained, having regard to the nature of the proceedings and the human rights implications of the client being unrepresented. It is not, however, the place of a solicitor ultimately to dissuade parents from seeking to oppose an order relating to their own child, if that is their instruction.

5.4 SEPARATE REPRESENTATION

5.4.1 Solicitors should be alert to whether separate representation of the adult party (non-parent or person with parental responsibility) can be justified in each case (see para. 2.7.2). Solicitors should generally consider whether their client's case can be adequately put to the court or if there is good reason for them to be joined as a party. This can be a complex issue (Professional Ethics on 0870 606 2577 may be able to assist).

5.5 CONFLICTS OF INTEREST

5.5.1 Solicitors should be alert to one or both of the parents presenting themselves as a unit and not recognising issues between them which may require separate representation.

5.5.2 Conversely over-representation where there is no conflict should be avoided (see also para. 2.7.2). This can be a complex issue (Professional Ethics on 0870 606 2577 may be able to assist).

5.6 CONFIDENTIALITY

5.6.1 Solicitors should be aware of and, in appropriate circumstances, must make clients aware of, the effect of Principle 16.02, Note 4 of the Guide, which states the exceptional circumstances in which solicitors should consider revealing confidential information to an appropriate authority:

> 'There may be exceptional circumstances involving children where a solicitor should consider revealing confidential information to an appropriate authority. This may be where the child is the client and the child reveals information which indicates continuing sexual or other physical abuse but refuses to allow disclosure of such information. Similarly, there may be situations

where an adult discloses abuse either by himself or herself or by another adult against a child but refuses to allow any disclosure. The solicitor must consider whether the threat to the child's life or health, both mental and physical, is sufficiently serious to justify a breach of the duty of confidentiality.'

5.6.2   It may also be necessary to breach confidentiality against the client's wishes in the following circumstances:

(a)   There is a duty to disclose reports obtained in the course of proceedings, even if adverse (Guide, Principle 16.02, Note 5).

(b)   In relation to disclosure of adverse material not obtained within the course of proceedings, in exceptional cases where to do otherwise would breach the solicitor's duty not to mislead the court (Guide, Principle 16.02, Note 5).

(c)   Where the solicitor is summoned as a witness or subpoenaed, the court may direct the solicitor to disclose documentation or divulge information.

5.6.3   However, solicitors should always bear in mind that they owe a duty of confidentiality to their clients and may have to justify any breach of that duty to their professional body. It is always advisable to seek advice from Professional Ethics (telephone 0870 606 2577), mentors, other members of the profession, partners in the firm and/or professional insurers.

5.7   THE CONDUCT OF CASES

5.7.1   Solicitors for parents and others should ensure that the client and the professionals involved are informed of their involvement and all other relevant details.

5.7.2   Clients should be kept informed throughout the case of the state and stage of the proceedings, and the reasons for and implications of any changes in the local authority's plans or delays.

5.7.3   Solicitors should advise the client about the possibility of parallel (or twin-track) planning, as appropriate. It is helpful to explain the local authority's duty from the outset to consider and assess alternative carers in case children cannot live at home in the future, and reassure the client as appropriate. A preferable outcome may be for the child to be placed with extended family. Clients should be encouraged to provide information to assist the local authority and the children's guardian in investigating alternatives within the family in the event of the child not being able to live at home. Solicitors should also explain to their clients the local authority's obligation to seek to locate non-resident parents.

5.7.4   Solicitors should bring to the attention of the court and other parties, as early as possible in the proceedings, issues related to language and communication difficulties, including requests for interpreter facilities and other 'special measures' to meet the client's particular needs in giving and listening to evidence.

5.7.5   Solicitors must advise their clients about the need for confidentiality in proceedings relating to children, and the fact that no documents produced for proceedings relating to children, including any expert reports and the report of the children's guardian, may be disclosed to those who are not parties to the proceedings without permission of the court.

5.7.6   Solicitors should advise clients on the need (if any) for witnesses, and should discourage clients from a proliferation of witnesses who add nothing to the case.

5.7.7   Solicitors should not interview children who are the subject of any case in which they are advising unless they are acting for the child who is a separate party to the proceedings. Parents who come to give instructions often have no one else to care for their children. Solicitors must be aware that it is usually inappropriate for instructions to be given in front of children who understand what is being said.

5.7.8   Solicitors should draft statements using the client's own words where possible, but avoid using emotive and/or inflammatory language, and/or expressing subjective opinions. They should ensure that statements drafted reflect the client's instructions.

5.7.9   Clients will need explanations of the roles of the other parties and professionals involved in the case, for example the children's guardian and of the role of the court. CAFCASS offices have supplies of explanatory leaflets.

5.7.10   Solicitors should also ensure that clients understand what will happen when they attend court. Before every hearing, the solicitor should discuss with the client whether the client is required, or whether it would be desirable, for him or her to attend the hearing. Solicitors should check their client's arrangements for getting to court and assist them in making arrangements as necessary. Giving evidence can be a very challenging experience. Time must be taken to explain to the client what is involved without actually rehearsing the evidence to be given.

5.7.11   They should seek to ensure that full cooperation is given to the children's guardian in the performance of his or her duties. Clients should be advised of the role of the children's guardian in the decision-making process, and the importance of his or her report. Solicitors should encourage clients to co-operate with the children's guardian and advise them that failure to do so could prejudice their case. Solicitors should consider, where appropriate and with the client's consent, copying correspondence to the children's guardian which has been sent on behalf of a parent or other adult party.

5.7.12   Solicitors should advise their clients that the child's solicitor may wish to interview the child, for example where the child is directly instructing the solicitor or where no children's guardian is available. If the child is living with the client they should be advised that the child's solicitor (or indeed the children's guardian) is likely to wish to see the child alone and the importance of this.

5.7.13   All correspondence in child care cases should be dealt with promptly.

5.7.14   Solicitors should have regard to Principle 16.06 of the Guide in relation to their duty to disclose all relevant information to their client unless the imparting of information to the client could be harmful to the client. This is a matter of professional judgement in each case. Speaking to a senior colleague or Children Panel solicitor may be of help.

5.7.15   Solicitors should always consider the most appropriate method of communicating sensitive or distressing information to their clients. For example, it may be appropriate to ask clients to come into the office to discuss the contents of a report, rather than forwarding it to their address without preparation or advice.

5.7.16 At the conclusion of proceedings, solicitors should consider seeking leave for disclosure of materials filed in the proceedings, for example in relation to an outstanding complaint under the Children Act 1989, s.26. Documentation may also be relevant for the purposes of treatment of an adult party, or to assist other relatives now caring for the child.

5.7.17 Solicitors should be aware that the timing of when complaints are made under the Children Act 1989, s.26 can affect the conduct of the case. It will be difficult for social services to respond where proceedings and a complaint investigation are under way at the same time. It is good practice to put the local authority on notice that a s.26 complaint is anticipated, and to air matters as appropriate within the proceedings; however, resolution is likely to be after the conclusion of proceedings.

5.8   EXPERTS

5.8.1 In proceedings under the Children Act 1989, solicitors are under a duty to disclose expert and other reports commissioned in the course of proceedings. The client should therefore be warned before instructing an expert of the risks involved in seeking reports which may contain adverse information or opinion (see the Guide, Principle 16.02, Note 5). The client needs to be warned that a solicitor is an officer of the court, and an advocate cannot mislead the court by act or omission, therefore such documents may have to be disclosed even if adverse. Where all parties agree to jointly instruct an expert, no specific permission is required from the court to disclose the papers to that expert. However, where there is no consensus to instruct an expert, the party seeking to adduce such evidence should make an 'on notice' application to the court requesting not only disclosure of papers, but permission to instruct their expert.

5.8.2 Solicitors should ensure that the right type of expert to assess an adult is appointed: for example, an adult psychiatrist as opposed to a child psychiatrist should conduct an adult psychiatric assessment.

5.8.3   Parent clients can be reluctant to share their medical notes with experts, fearing that their past medical history will damage their case. Solicitors must remember their duty not to mislead the court. They should be prepared to advise clients that their concerns can be overcome where appropriate, and that the sharing of information can be of benefit to their case. In some cases, only the expert needs see the notes. The client should be advised of the likely view to be taken by the court if the client does not agree to disclosure.

5.9   AFTER CONCLUSION OF PROCEEDINGS

5.9.1   Solicitors must write to clients confirming the outcome of proceedings and return, where available, any original documents which clients have provided.

5.9.2   Solicitors must remind clients of the continuing confidential nature of the proceedings and any relevant documents.

5.9.3   Solicitors should explain to clients what contact they will have with the child. They should be advised to contact their solicitor if contact is not offered as provided for in the care plan, or if changes are made in relation to contact.

5.9.4   Solicitors should consider the need for making a CICA claim where the child is placed with their client.

5.9.5   Solicitors should be aware of any support and specialist services which should be made available to clients in relation to problems underlying the causes of removal of the child, and removal itself, including counselling.

5.9.6   Solicitors should advise the client of the local authority's future responsibilities to them and the child. These will vary depending whether the outcome was a care order, a supervision order, a s.8 order or no order. The child may remain a child in need within the meaning of the Children Act 1989, s.17. Solicitors should advise as to:

(a)   the importance of the care plan;

(b)   the parents' right to be invited to meetings that seek to make fundamental changes to the care plans where children are subject to care orders;

(c)   where appropriate, the documentation and information on the child which they should expect to receive;

(d)   statutory reviews.

5.9.7   Clients should be advised to attend every six-monthly review and of the proposed dates, if already fixed by the local authority. This will assist in the mechanism for reviewing and spotting 'breaches' of the care plan. They should be advised to expect issues of contact and discharge of the care order to be covered at every review. They should raise any omission of these items at the meeting.

5.9.8   Solicitors should advise clients to retain all future documentation and information on the child received, which may be of importance in the future and to any future proceedings.

5.9.9   The importance of the care plan should be emphasised to clients. Solicitors should advise on the mechanism for reviewing the court's decisions and the circumstances in which it would be appropriate to apply for discharge of a care order or for variation of contact, as appropriate. Solicitors should advise as to the steps the local authority will take in considering whether to apply to extend a supervision order on its expiry.

5.9.10   Regard should be had to the Law Society's guidance on ownership storage and destruction of documents contained in the Guide, possibly to the child's 24th birthday, or until the youngest child who is the subject of the proceedings has attained majority.

PART 6

Other important aspects of public law Children Act cases

6.1 SECURE ACCOMMODATION

6.1.1 The court cannot make a secure accommodation order unless the child's solicitor has the opportunity of taking instructions from the child and the child has been granted the minimum rights contained in ECHR, Art. 6(3) (see *Re AS (Secure Accommodation Order)* (1999) 1 FLR 103 and *Re C (Secure Accommodation Order: Representation)* (2001) 2 FLR 169). It is essential that all solicitors dealing with a secure accommodation application have regard to the Department of Health guidance *The Children Act Guidance and Regulations: Vol 1 Court Orders* (HMSO, 1991), the Children (Secure Accommodation) Regulations 1991 (SI 1991/1505) and the Children (Secure Accommodation) (No.2) Regulations 1991 (SI 1991/2034). The welfare checklist applies but the child's welfare, although relevant, is not paramount in these proceedings (see *Re M (a minor) (Secure Accommodation Order)* [1995] 1 FLR 418, *Re W (a minor) (Secure Accommodation Order)* [1993] 1 FLR 692, *Re B (a minor)* [1994] 2 FLR 707, *Re C* v. *Humberside County Council and another* [1994] 2 FLR 759).

6.1.2 Solicitors will probably only have a few hours' notice of an appointment to act for a child on a secure accommodation application. Solicitors should consider how instructions will be obtained and confirm the arrangements for the child's attendance at court. Solicitors should try to ensure the child is brought to court as early as possible in order to allow time for the taking of instructions, but through liaison with the court ensure that the matter is heard promptly to avoid unnecessary waiting time, particularly if the court facilities are inadequate.

Solicitors should check in advance with the court and the secure unit to ensure that children will not be kept in cells before the hearing, nor be admitted to the court through the cells and make representations as necessary.

6.1.3 It is possible that the solicitor's first meeting with the child will be at court. The solicitor for the child should assess initially whether the child is of sufficient age and understanding to give instructions. The issue of separate representation for the child and the children's guardian may arise. Where the child is of sufficient age and understanding to give instructions it is likely that the child's solicitor will no longer act on the instructions of the children's guardian.

6.1.4 The evidence should be rigorously tested by all the parties since the serious issue of the child's liberty is at stake.

6.1.5 Continuity of representation for all parties is necessary in secure accommodation applications, since the orders are frequently made after adjournment. Continuity of representation for the child is vital.

6.1.6 Solicitors must have particular regard to ECHR, Art. 5 (right to liberty and security).

6.1.7 Solicitors should also have regard to the age of the child. Where the child is under 13 secure accommodation proceedings should not be begun without the permission of the Secretary of State. This should be confirmed with the local authority. If an accommodated child over 16 seeks to discharge himself or herself from secure accommodation, consideration should be given to making an application for a care order. On transfer up of a care application those proceedings are 'pending in another court' under the Children (Allocation of Proceedings) Order 1991, Art. 7(3) so as to found jurisdiction upon which to transfer the secure accommodation application, and in practice such proceedings are normally consolidated.

6.2 CONTACT WITH LOOKED AFTER CHILDREN

6.2.1 Early consideration should be given to the issue of contact, including sibling contact as well as contact between the child and parents and any other significant person in the child's life.

Interim care plans should address these contact issues. Solicitors for the other parties must be alert as to whether the issue of contact has been addressed.

6.2.2   Any contact centres used should be suitable to meet the safety needs of the child and family.

6.2.3   Solicitors should ensure that in all cases where contact is suspended without an order under the Children Act 1989, s.34(4), the case is returned to court even if the suspension is agreed.

6.2.4   After the making of a care order, if any departure from the plan in relation to contact is proposed at any stage, local authority solicitors should remind the social worker to discuss this with the parties. If the parents or family are concerned that the plan in relation to contact is not being followed, attempts should be made to discuss and settle this with the local authority. It may be helpful for the local authority to be the party making any necessary application to the court.

6.3   ADOPTION

6.3.1   Solicitors are asked to note that at the time of writing of this guidance, relevant parts of the Adoption and Children Act 2002 were not implemented. Solicitors should seek to keep themselves informed of developments on the inter-relationship between care proceedings and the placement provisions in the Adoption and Children Act 2002.

6.3.2   Solicitors are referred in particular to the guidance 'Adoption Proceedings – A New Approach', issued by the President of the Family Division and available at **www.courtservice.gov.uk/cms/ media/a20b.pdf**; and the National Adoption Standards issued by the Department of Health and in force since April 2003, available at **www.doh.gov.uk/adoption** which made changes to previous guidance, including that contained in 'Care Plans and Care Proceedings under the Children Act 1989' (LAC (99) 29).

6.3.3   The inter-relationship between care proceedings and adoption is a complex one and practice varies from area to area, particularly with regard to the use of freeing applications. A degree of standardisation of practice may develop with the introduction of the Protocol.

6.3.4 Parallel (or twin-track) planning should be used where adoption is under consideration. It is an important part of the process in avoiding delay. However, before reaching a decision that adoption should be the principal aim of the care plan, the local authority must be satisfied that sufficient assessment has taken place to rule out rehabilitation or placement with relatives, for example under a residence order.

6.3.5 Under the provisions of the Adoption Agencies Regulations 1983 (SI 1983/1964), there is a staged process involved in adoption planning by the local authority. The local authority's adoption panel must consider:

(a) whether adoption is in the best interests of a child (the 'best interests' recommendation);

(b) if so, whether a freeing application should be made; and

(c) whether a prospective adopter would be a suitable adoptive parent for a particular child (the 'matching' recommendation).

6.3.6 Where adoption is the probable option, the courts will need to be advised of the key steps and estimated timescales to implement such a plan. Lack of such information could result in serious delay before placement, and is detrimental to the child's welfare.

6.3.7 The National Adoption Standards provide that an adoptive placement should be identified within six months of the *conclusion* of the care proceedings. The practice of requiring detailed evidence during care proceedings of a family finding programme causes delay, and diverts family finding social workers from their principal task, and so is to be avoided.

6.3.8 The amount of progress made before the final hearing will depend on a range of factors, including the overall timescale of the care proceedings. In addition, sensitivity is needed to ensure that the child's parents understand that the care hearing is not the same as any later hearing under adoption legislation, which would need to address questions of parental consent, unless a freeing application is being considered at the same time.

6.3.9 Where the local authority has ruled out rehabilitation or placement with relatives and has confirmed adoption as the preferred option, the following should always be addressed before the final hearing:

(a) identification of the key steps and timetable leading to an adoptive placement;

(b) preparation of the BAAF Form E;

(c) that the Adoption Panel should consider the case with a view to making a 'best interests' recommendation;

(d) whether a freeing application is appropriate.

6.3.10 It is not appropriate before the final care hearing for there to have been introductions between the child and the prospective adopters, or for the agency to have confirmed the panel's recommendations.

6.3.11 Where simultaneous freeing and care proceedings are appropriate, local authority solicitors should advise their 'clients' on coordination of evidence and timetabling of the court hearings.

6.3.12 If a final care order is made with an adoption care plan and no freeing order has been made, the local authority solicitor should ask the court for a direction that papers in the care proceedings be released to prospective adopters.

6.3.13 The findings of fact made in the care proceedings are often of importance in later adoption proceedings. Accordingly, if the judgment or reasons are not given in writing, consideration should also be given to whether a transcript should be obtained and who should pay for it. If a transcript is not made available, at the very least the advocates should agree a note of the findings of fact in the care proceedings.

6.3.14 Where a care order with an adoption care plan or a freeing order has been made in the High Court, the local authority solicitor should consider seeking the direction that a future application for an adoption order may be filed in a county court of the prospective adopter's choice. This may avoid future delay.

6.3.15 Solicitors are referred to the notice in *Focus 42* (July 2003) relating to local authority funding to support adoption proceedings.

6.4 DISCHARGE AND VARIATION OF CARE/SUPERVISION ORDERS

6.4.1 Local authority solicitors should be mindful of the need for their client to keep the appropriateness of the care order under review.

6.4.2 Where a care order is no longer appropriate or is lapsed in practice, the local authority should apply for discharge of the care order in a timely manner, not wait for the adult parties or the child to make an application.

6.4.3 Where another party is considering applying for discharge of the care order, initially this should be discussed, if possible, with the local authority. It may be possible to reach agreement before referral back to the court. This also gives opportunity for the parties to consider whether it would be better if the local authority made the application.

6.4.4 When considering an application for discharge of a care order, consideration should be given as to whether the issue of the leaving care plan for eligible children has been adequately addressed, including the question of referral to adult services for the child at 18.

6.4.5 An application to extend a supervision order should be made in a timely manner in order to avoid an eleventh hour application before expiry.

Protocol for Judicial Case Management in Public Law Children Act Cases: 'Route Map – The 6 Steps'

1

The Application

Day 1 to Day 3

Objective:
LA to provide sufficient information to identify issues/make early welfare and case management decisions

Action:

- LA file Application in Form C1/C13 on Day 1 [1.1]

- Directions on Issue by Court
  - fixing first hearing
  - Appointment of Guardian on Day 1 [1.2]

- Allocation of Guardian by Cafcass by Day 3 [1.2-3]

- Appointment of Solicitor for the child
  - no appointment of Guardian
  - Notification to parties of name of Guardian/solicitor on Day 3 [1.4]

- LA File and serve Documents by Day 3 [1.5]

2

The First Hearing in the FPC

On (or before) Day 6

Objective:
To decide what immediate steps are necessary/ contested ICO/preventing delay/appropriate court

Action:

- Parties [2.2]

- Contested Interim Care Orders [2.3]

- Transfer [2.4] and transfer arrangements [2.5]

- Initial Case Management and Checklist [2.6] including:
  - Case Management Conference
  - Final Hearing
  - Pre-Hearing Review
  - Evidence
  - Disclosure
  - Core Assessment
  - Standard Directions Form

by Day 6

5 days

3

Allocation Hearing & Directions

By Day 11(CC) 15(HC)

Objective:
To make provision for continuous/consistent judicial case management

Action:

Care Centre court officer shall:

- Allocate 1-2 Judges (including final hearing judge) [3.2]

- Attach SDF with proposed date for CMC, Final Hearing and PHR by Day 8 [3.2]:

Judge (at Allocation Hearing) considers:

- Transfer, ICO, CM Checklist, dates for CMC,Final Hearing, PHR, Disclosure, Core Assessment, SDF by Day 11 [3.4]

- Case Management Documents [3.4]

 1 day

In High Court:

- Court Officer by Day 12 [3.6]

- Case Management Judge by Day 15 [3.7]

Within 54 days

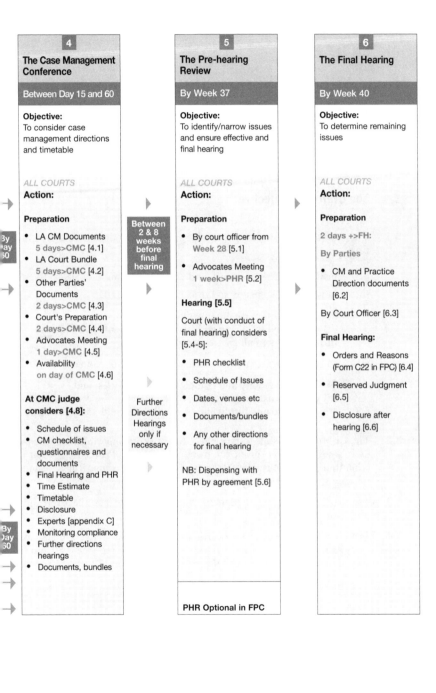

4

The Case Management Conference

Between Day 15 and 60

Objective:
To consider case management directions and timetable

ALL COURTS
Action:

Preparation

- LA CM Documents
  5 days>CMC [4.1]
- LA Court Bundle
  5 days>CMC [4.2]
- Other Parties' Documents
  2 days>CMC [4.3]
- Court's Preparation
  2 days>CMC [4.4]
- Advocates Meeting
  1 day>CMC [4.5]
- Availability
  on day of CMC [4.6]

At CMC judge considers [4.8]:

- Schedule of issues
- CM checklist, questionnaires and documents
- Final Hearing and PHR
- Time Estimate
- Timetable
- Disclosure
- Experts [appendix C]
- Monitoring compliance
- Further directions hearings
- Documents, bundles

By Day 60

By Day 60

Between 2 & 8 weeks before final hearing

Further Directions Hearings only if necessary

5

The Pre-hearing Review

By Week 37

Objective:
To identify/narrow issues and ensure effective and final hearing

ALL COURTS
Action:

Preparation

- By court officer from Week 28 [5.1]
- Advocates Meeting
  1 week>PHR [5.2]

Hearing [5.5]

Court (with conduct of final hearing) considers [5.4-5]:

- PHR checklist
- Schedule of Issues
- Dates, venues etc
- Documents/bundles
- Any other directions for final hearing

NB: Dispensing with PHR by agreement [5.6]

PHR Optional in FPC

6

The Final Hearing

By Week 40

Objective:
To determine remaining issues

ALL COURTS
Action:

Preparation

2 days +>FH:

By Parties

- CM and Practice Direction documents [6.2]

By Court Officer [6.3]

Final Hearing:

- Orders and Reasons (Form C22 in FPC) [6.4]
- Reserved Judgment [6.5]
- Disclosure after hearing [6.6]

Overriding objective of the Protocol – from *Practice Direction (Care Cases: Judicial Continuity and Judicial Case Management)*

3 The Overriding Objective

3.1 The overriding objective is to enable the Court to deal with every care case

(a) justly, expeditiously, fairly and with the minimum of delay;

(b) in ways which ensure, so far as is practicable, that

    (i) the parties are on an equal footing;

    (ii) the welfare of the children involved is safeguarded; and

    (iii) distress to all parties is minimised;

(c) so far as is practicable, in ways which are proportionate

    (i) to the gravity and complexity of the issues; and

    (ii) to the nature and extent of the intervention proposed in the private and family life of the children and adults involved.

3.2 The Court should seek to give effect to the overriding objective when it exercises any power given to it by the Family Proceedings Courts (Children Act 1989) Rules 1991 or the Family Proceedings Rules 1991 (as the case may be) or interprets any rule.

3.3 The parties are required to help the Court to further the overriding objective.

3.4 The Court will further the overriding objective by actively managing cases as required by sections 11 and 32 of the Children Act 1989 and in accordance with the Practice Direction, Principles and Protocol.

Accessing solicitor and Children Panel information

The Law Society holds a database of all solicitors in England and Wales. All information about solicitors is sourced from this database. It includes the solicitor's practising details and any qualifications or accreditation, for example, as a member of the Law Society's Children Panel.

Currently there are a number of ways to access up-to-date details about solicitors, including membership of Law Society panels:

- The Law Society's Information Services: call 01527 504433 or write to the Law Society Information Services at the address below.

- Solicitors Online (**www.solicitors-online.com**): this is the Law Society's online search engine to find solicitors and panel members. Enter post-code, select which panel you need and it will give you a list of up to 100 nearest firms with telephone numbers.

- Yellow pages directory display blocks: solicitors opt to pay for inclusion in a block with the Law Society logo displaying membership of Law Society panels.

- Mailing lists: commercial lists may be requested through the Law Society's *Gazette* office by faxing 020 7320 5966.

THE LAW SOCIETY'S CHILDREN PANEL

Full current membership lists for Children Representatives, Adult Party Representatives and Local Authority Representatives are regularly posted at **www.panels.lawsociety.org.uk** within the Children Panel section.

The Law Society
Information Services
Ipsley Court
Berrington Close
Redditch, Worcs
B98 0TD

DX 19114 Redditch
Tel: 020 7242 1222
Fax: 01527 510213
Email: panels@lawsociety.org.uk

Types of expert

WHAT TYPE OF EXPERT IS REQUIRED?

The most common experts in care cases are likely to be:

- Paediatrician: to carry out or comment on development; causation and dating of injuries; long term prognosis
- Paediatric haematologist: to advise on the causes of bleeding
- Paediatric neuroradiologist: for skull fractures and subdurals
- Paediatric neurosurgeon: to deal with subdural haematomas
- Ophthalmologist: for retinal haemorrhages
- Paediatric radiologist: to read the skeletal survey, MRI scan and/or CT scan
- Paediatric metabolic consultant: to test for any metabolic disorder
- Haematologist: to look at possible bleeding disorders
- Forensic pathologist: their exclusive experience is with death in suspicious circumstances; will conduct a post mortem and reach a decision as to the cause of death, and whether the explanation given is plausible
- Geneticist: may be able to provide an answer as to the possibility of a chromosomal abnormality, gene deficiency, or a rare syndrome.

There has been little consistency over the country in the way that psychiatrists and psychologists are used in care cases: in some parts of the country it is invariably a psychiatrist who is brought in as an expert, on parenting ability, attachment, contact issues; in others it is always a psychologist. However they have different skills:

- A psychiatrist has expertise in terms of specialist knowledge of mental illness and personality disorders.
- A psychologist has expertise in general functioning and management of life's responsibilities.

WHICH EXPERT?

Care must be taken in the choice of any expert. The questions to be addressed will include:

- whether the CV indicates an expertise in the particular field which is relevant, for example:

    - a doctor qualified as a physician may have acquired knowledge as to the psychological aspects of the work, but would usually not be qualified to give a psychological or psychiatric opinion
    - an adult psychiatrist will not usually be regarded as sufficiently expert in the field of psychological medicine to be called as an expert in that field
    - a bio-chemist cannot give an opinion as a paediatrician;

- whether there has been any reported judicial criticism of the proposed expert;

- whether the expert has acknowledged a leaning towards a particular view;

- whether s/he usually gets in the report on time;

- how difficult it is to arrange for him/her to attend court hearings for a block period;

- whether the expert is suitable given case sensitive issues such as allegations of sexual abuse, the gender of the child/ren, ethnicity, language, religion.

Data protection and social services

KEY LEGISLATION

Data Protection Act 1998

Data Protection (Subject Access Modification) (Health) Order 2000,
SI 2000/413

Data Protection (Subject Access Modification) (Education) Order 2000,
SI 2000/414

Data Protection (Subject Access Modification) (Social Work) Order 2000,
SI 2000/415

Data Protection (Processing of Sensitive Personal Data) Order 2000,
SI 2000/417

Data Protection (Miscellaneous Subject Access Exemptions) Order 2000,
SI 2000/419

Data Protection (Miscellaneous Subject Access Exemptions) (Amendment)
Order 2000, SI 2000/1865

DATA PROTECTION

- There must be best practice in recording information on social services files based on key principles of partnership, openness and accuracy.
- Social services should have a policy framework that expresses the values and principles underpinning recording practice. There should be a statement of purpose of recording, definition of documents to be routinely copied to users, statements of access, public information on social services policy and practice and agreements on information provided by other agencies.
- All personal data must be adequate, relevant and not excessive for the purpose for which it is held, kept up to date and not kept for longer than is necessary for its purpose.

RIGHT OF ACCESS

- Subject to a limited number of exemptions, any living person who is the subject of personal information held and processed by a social services authority has a right of access to that data.

- A person does not have the right to know what is recorded about someone else, i.e. a family member, without that person's consent. There may be cases where it is reasonable in all the circumstances to comply without that other person's consent.

- Where a child or young person under the age of 18 makes a request for access to records, the authority will need to decide whether or not he or she has sufficient understanding to do so.

- If the child or young person does not have sufficient understanding to make his or her own request, a person with parental responsibility can make the request. The authority should be satisfied that the child lacks capacity to make the application or has capacity and has authorised the parent to make the application. The authority needs to be satisfied the request made by the parent on the child's behalf is in the child's interest.

- No special provision is made about requests for access made on behalf of an adult who lacks mental capacity and is incapable of managing their own affairs.

- An agent may make a valid request for access on behalf of the data subject. Written authority should normally be provided by the agent.

- The Act applies only to data about living persons. However, there may still be issues of confidentiality surrounding access to records about a deceased person.

- A request for access has to be made in writing and accompanied by the appropriate fee, subject to a maximum £10.

- Access can be refused where the authority has previously complied with an identical or similar request from the same individual, unless a reasonable interval has elapsed in between.

- Any information should be given in an intelligible manner, providing a permanent copy of the information.

- The information should usually be provided within 40 days from receipt of the written request and appropriate fee.

- The data subject may ask the data controller to correct any inaccurate information. This means incorrect or misleading as to any matter of fact as opposed to opinion.

EXEMPTIONS

- Prevention or detection of crime.
- Where disclosure to the data subject would be likely to prejudice the carrying out of social work by causing serious harm to the physical or mental health or condition, of the data subject or another person.
- The local authority must not disclose information about physical or mental health or condition without first consulting an appropriate health professional, i.e. GP or psychiatrist.
- Where other enactments themselves prevent disclosure, then a data subject cannot rely on the Data Protection Act to seek access to records, i.e. adoption records and reports.

CHALLENGING REFUSAL

- The authority should record the reasons for its decision and explain these to the data subject. Reasons should be given as soon as practicable and in writing.
- The data subject may appeal to the courts or Data Protection Commissioner. The court has power to order disclosure.
- The Commissioner may issue enforcement notices for breach of data protection principles.
- There is a right of appeal to the Data Protection Tribunal against an enforcement notice.

DISCLOSURE TO OTHER AGENCIES

- The authority may disclose information with the consent of the data subject.
- It is necessary to ensure the processing is fair and lawful.
- Where disclosure of data is necessary to comply with a legal obligation imposed on an authority, then the consent of the data subject is not necessary. The data subject should be informed that such an obligation exists.
- An authority may disclose personal information to social services staff directly involved in a case and their line managers. They may also disclose personal information to anyone else who cares for one of their clients, i.e. a voluntary body or foster carers or any independent providers.
- Volunteers and informal carers may also need to be given some personal information about the data subject.

- Other organisations may also require personal information to discharge their statutory functions, i.e. health, education, inspection/audit, legal advisors, local authority finance staff and police.

- The local authority may be required to disclose information to other bodies. Examples are disclosure of information to the police, courts, tribunals, statutory inquiries, Secretary of State for Health, children's guardians, health and safety executive. Where disclosure is ordered by the courts, social services are advised by the Department of Health to take professional and legal advice and that any information disclosed should be the minimum necessary to meet the requirements of the situation. The authority should record its reasons for disclosure.

CIRCULARS AND FURTHER INFORMATION

Local Authority Social Services Letter (2000) 2

Data Protection Act 1998: Guidance to Social Services (March 2000) at **www.doh.gov.uk/scg/datap.htm**

Department of Health Social Care Group 2A, Room 624, Wellington House, 133–155 Waterloo Road, London SE1 8UG

Tel: 020 79724160

Data Protection Commissioner Office, Wycliffe House, Water Lane, Wilmslow, Cheshire, SK9 5AF

Tel: (information line) 01625 545 745

www.dataprotection.gov.uk

Code of Guidance for Disclosure of Police Information in Family Proceedings (ACPO pilot code)

OBJECTIVE

The objective of this Code of Guidance is to set out the mechanism agreed between the Greater Manchester Police Authority and the Manchester Care Centre to provide the Court with early information to enable it to properly determine any necessary direction(s) to be made in relation to documents, records or other evidential material held by the police in relevant criminal proceedings or investigation which may inform the court (and the parties) in the determination of any factual or welfare issue within family proceedings, and:

- To provide timely advance notice to the Police Authority and the police of the existence of the family proceedings and the nature and detail of the information sought from the police

- To enable the police through the Police Authority to indicate in advance what documents, records or other evidential material (including both used and unused material) is or may be available to be disclosed to the family court and whether there is any objection to or difficulty in the immediate disclosure of the same

- To assist the court (and the parties) in the framing of standard directions directed to the Police Authority which will act as the conduit to process and deal with all such directions affecting each Division of the Greater Manchester Police without any undue delay

- To encourage early disclosure of full and frank information between the police, the parties and the Court subject only to the avoidance of prejudice to the proper conduct of ongoing police enquiries at the time of the request.

Action	Party	Timing
1. Preparation for Request for Disclosure *1.1 Preliminary Enquiries of Police* Not later than 12 days before the relevant hearing the solicitors for any party who proposes to ask the Court for a direction requiring the Chief Constable of any Police Authority to disclose within family proceedings any document, record or other evidential material shall approach the police solicitor at the **Greater Manchester Police Criminal Justice Department Civil Unit** with the following information: • The names and dates of birth of the parties including any relevant children and where possible, brief details of the circumstances of the incident(s) in respect of which the request is made • Any relevant addresses • The date of the specific incident or incidents upon which information is sought • The crime reference number (if known) • The name and collar number (if known) of the Officer(s) in the case(s) • The nature of the documents, records or other evidential material sought or the likelihood of any request to be made for all documents, records or other evidential material to be disclosed • The date of the hearing at which the formal direction is to be sought • A draft of the proposed direction including the date by which the documents, records or other evidential material is likely to be directed to be disclosed (to be prepared in accordance with Standard Variable Directions wherever possible) • The likely timetable of legal and social work steps • Whether and if so what date has been fixed by the court for any final hearing or fact finding hearing and whether the officer in the case is likely to be required at that hearing to give evidence	The party proposing direction for disclosure of police evidence	12 days before relevant hearing

Action	Party	Timing
1.2 Police Response Not later than 7 days before the relevant hearing the solicitors for the party proposing the direction be made for disclosure of documents, records or other evidential material shall obtain from the police solicitor at the Criminal Justice Department Civil Unit, the following information: ● What documents, records or other evidential material are available in relation to the subject matter of the request for disclosure (if any) ● If the police are not able to provide this information, the reason(s) why and when it is anticipated that the information can be provided ● Whether the documents, records or other evidential material can be provided within the timescale proposed by the draft direction provided ● If the documents, records or other evidential material can not be provided within the timescale proposed by the draft direction, the reason why they can not be so provided and the timescale requested by the police for their disclosure ● Whether the police require the direction in relation to disclosure to be amended as to its terms from the draft provided, and if so in what terms do the police propose that the direction should be framed ● Where it is indicated that a police officer may be required to give evidence at any hearing, when that police officer is available to give evidence, and the dates and/or times to avoid.	The Party proposing direction for disclosure of police evidence	7 days before relevant hearing
2. The Hearing At the hearing where the request is made for disclosure the court shall consider: ● The necessity and relevance to the issues required to be determined by the court, of the information sought to be disclosed ● The wording of the proposed direction for disclosure, with reference to Standard Variable Directions wherever possible		

• The timing of any direction for disclosure with specific reference to any representations made in that regard by the police • The making of a request to the Family Division Manager that the court order be expedited in its preparation in accordance with the process described in the Schedule hereto and served within 24 hours by the court upon the police solicitor at the Criminal Justice Department Civil Unit • Any necessary direction to the party making the request for disclosure, as to notice and service of the court order in accordance with this Protocol.		

3. Post-Hearing Action

3.1 The solicitor securing the direction in respect of disclosure shall forthwith comply with the process described in the Schedule hereto and thereafter ensure that within 24 hours of the hearing the police solicitor is aware of the terms of the direction made for disclosure.	The Party securing direction for disclosure	Within 24 hours of directions hearing
3.2 The solicitor securing the direction in respect of disclosure shall forthwith upon receipt of the court order and in any event within 2 days of the hearing serve the court order upon the police solicitor at the Criminal Justice Department Civil Unit.	The Party securing direction for disclosure	Within 2 days of directions hearing

SCHEDULE TO PROTOCOL FOR DISCLOSURE OF POLICE EVIDENCE

Following the relevant directions hearing the solicitors securing the direction for disclosure shall forthwith either

(a) obtain immediately from the court clerk a sealed copy of the order in the terms approved; or

(b) attend at the court office with the approved order in the terms agreed (or, if attendance at the court office is not immediately practical send a copy by Fax) and arrange with the Family Division Manager (or such other representative of the court service as the Family Division Manager shall nominate) for the order to be drawn up and sealed immediately.

In any event the order shall be made available to the party securing it to enable compliance with Protocol steps 3.1 and 3.2.

The address for service of any order is –

The Greater Manchester Police Force Solicitor
Criminal Justice Department Civil Unit
PO Box 47 (S West PDO)
Chester House
Boyer Street
Manchester M16 0RE
Tel: 0161 856 1689/ Fax: 0161 856 2733

Sample protocol on exchange of information

A PROTOCOL BETWEEN THE CROWN PROSECUTION SERVICE POLICE AND LOCAL AUTHORITIES IN THE EXCHANGE OF INFORMATION IN THE INVESTIGATION AND PROSECUTION OF CHILD ABUSE CASES

1. Parties

1.1 The parties to this protocol are the [name of the Local Authority], [name of Police Force] and the Crown Prosecution Service.

2. Aim

2.1 The aim of this protocol is to provide an agreed framework between the parties for the sharing and exchange of relevant information in child protection enquiries for the purposes of criminal prosecutions in [specify Area].

3. Objectives

3.1 The objectives of this protocol are:

- To provide guidance in obtaining and sharing information between the Parties in order to protect the welfare of children by investigating and prosecuting offenders through the criminal justice system;
- To provide guidance that enables the Parties to apply a consistent approach to information sharing locally; and
- To foster a greater understanding between the Parties of their respective roles within the criminal justice system.

4.   Introduction

4.1   Good practice calls for effective co-operation between the parties; working in the best interests of the child; and careful exercise of professional judgment based on thorough assessment and analysis of relevant information. This protocol is addressed to those who work in the investigation and prosecution of offenders in relation to child abuse cases.

4.2   The Parties recognise the fundamental importance of inter-agency working in combating child abuse. The Parties are committed to share information and intelligence between them where this is necessary to protect children as set out in the document entitled *Working Together to Safeguard Children.*

4.3   This protocol recognises:

(a)   Social Services and Education departments of Local Authorities will always seek to act in the best interests of the children with whom they are involved; and

(b)   The Police and the Crown Prosecution Service are bound by a duty to protect the confidentiality of material held by Local Authorities (dealing with the appropriate Social Services or Education department) and will not disclose to third parties, except with the leave of the court, or with the consent of the Local Authority, any material obtained directly or indirectly as a result of having access to material held by Local Authorities.

5.   The legal framework

5.1   The duties of the Parties are set out in Annex A. The legal framework at Annex A, sets out the legal obligations, on which this protocol is based, of the Parties in relation to exchanging and sharing of information.

6.   Procedure

6.1   As soon as the Police investigating a suspected crime believe material exists within the Social Services and Education files which may be relevant to the investigation, they will notify the Local Authority by means of a written notice.

6.2   The Police will appoint, as appropriate, a suitably trained disclosure officer who will carry out the examination of relevant material on Social Services and Education files held by the Local Authority and whose task it will be to liaise with the Local Authority.

6.3   The written notice used by the police disclosure officer will include: (see attached draft letter at Annex B)

- The identity and contact details of the police disclosure officer;
- The identity and contact details of the officer in the case;
- A summary of the case and the details of the offences being investigated;
- A statement of the relevant information which is sought from the records in order to pursue all reasonable lines of enquiry, and why that information is thought likely to be relevant to the investigation;
- A statement of how failure to disclose relevant information would prejudice or delay the investigation.

6.4 Upon receipt of a request from the Police under 6.3, the Local Authority will appoint a suitably trained disclosure officer from the legal department who will liaise with the Police disclosure officer throughout the enquiry. The Local Authority disclosure officer will identify and collate relevant material from the Social Services/Education files which it is necessary to disclose for the purposes of the police investigation, in the light of the information provided by the Police in 6.3 above.[1] The review by the police will usually take place on Local Authority premises but may be elsewhere by agreement between the disclosure officers.

6.5 The Local Authority will ensure that documents filed in family court proceedings are not included in the files to be seen by the police and/or Crown Prosecution Service. Where there are documents filed in family court proceedings, the Local Authority will provide a list of that material without describing what it is, in order for the police, if appropriate, to apply to the Family Court for disclosure.

6.6 The Local Authority will not reveal to the police relevant medical reports or other medical information without the consent of the author of that material. Where there is such material, the Local Authority will seek consent from the author to reveal it to the police. Where consent is refused, the Local Authority will inform the police that the material exists. The police and the Crown Prosecution Service may seek consent from the author of the material and/or apply for a witness summons to obtain the material.

6.7 When the Local Authority voluntarily discloses material to the defence they will reveal it to the police and/or Crown Prosecution Service. In addition, when the defence request material from the Local Authority under the Data Protection Act 1998, the Local Authority will notify the police and/or Crown Prosecution Service of the fact of that request.

---

1   At this stage, the local authority will disclose to the police information that is relevant for the purposes of the police investigation. This does not mean that the local authority, by so doing, is agreeing that the information disclosed to the police should in due course be disclosed to the defence. Such disclosure will be decided either by agreement between the local authority and the CPS or in default of such an agreement, an order of the court made under the CPIA.

6.8 The Police disclosure officer will be given priority to review the material following the agreed [see above] working day period. If there are difficulties in complying with the agreed timescale or if the material is ready for review more quickly, the Local Authority disclosure officer will notify the Police disclosure officer immediately.

6.9 Where the Police review the material, the Local Authority will accept that the Police may take notes or copies of the material as appropriate, as they require for the purposes of their investigation. The Police will accept that any material they read and any notes or copies they take are to be regarded as sensitive material which is subject to public interest immunity.

6.10 Any material identified by the Police disclosure officer during the review as being relevant to the issues in any criminal proceedings which may undermine the prosecution case or may reasonably assist any apparent defence case, must be brought to the attention of the Local Authority disclosure officer with a view to the Police disclosure officer obtaining a copy of the relevant documents. Any copy documents provided by the Local Authority to the Police will be treated as sensitive material which is subject to public interest immunity.

6.11 When the Police submit a full file to the Crown Prosecution Service, including all correspondence between the Police and the Local Authority, the Police disclosure officer will identify all unused material on the appropriate (MG) forms and in particular material that is viewed and obtained from the Local Authority. It will be the duty of the Police disclosure officer to identify any material which might undermine the prosecution case or might reasonably assist the defence case.

6.12 In the event of further relevant material coming into the possession of the Social Services and Education departments, the Local Authority disclosure officer will disclose to the Police disclosure officer that material and will provide a continuous opportunity to review and take copies of that material. Further, it is accepted by the Local Authority that as an enquiry develops, the material may have to be re-visited.

6.13 On receipt of the full file the Crown Prosecution Service will review the unused material in accordance with its statutory duties under the Criminal Procedure and Investigations Act 1996 (CPIA).

6.14 The Crown Prosecution Service shall treat all material disclosed by the local Authority as sensitive material.

6.15 Where any Local Authority material reviewed by the Crown Prosecution Service falls within the statutory disclosure tests under the CPIA, the Crown Prosecution Service shall write to the Local Authority disclosure officer, within [ ] days of review, setting out the reasons why the material falls to be disclosed and informing them of that decision. Within [ ] days of receipt of that notification, the Local Authority disclosure officer shall be given an opportunity to make any representations in writing to the Crown Prosecution Service on the issues of disclosure.

6.16 The Crown Prosecution Service will not disclose any material to the defence unless by agreement with the Local Authority or by order of the court following a public interest immunity application.

6.17 If the Local Authority agrees with the Crown Prosecution Service to disclose material identified by the Crown Prosecution Service which falls within the statutory disclosure tests under the CPIA, the Crown Prosecution Service will disclose the material to the defence.

6.18 If the Local Authority asserts public interest immunity and objects to disclosure, to the defence, of any material identified by the Crown Prosecution Service which falls within the statutory disclosure tests under the CPIA, the Crown Prosecution Service will make a public interest immunity application to the court as soon as reasonably practical. The Crown Prosecution Service will notify the Local Authority of the date and venue of the public interest immunity application and inform the Local Authority of their rights to make representations to the court under the Crown Court (Criminal Procedure and Investigations Act 1996) (Disclosure) Rules 1997 and the Magistrates' Court (Criminal Procedure and Investigations Act 1996) (Disclosure) Rules 1997.

6.19 Following receipt of a defence statement, the Police disclosure officer will send a copy of the defence statement to the Local Authority disclosure officer.

6.20 The Local Authority disclosure officer will reconsider the relevance of the material held by the Local Authority in the light of the defence statement. Where the Local Authority identify further material to be revealed, the Local Authority disclosure officer will notify the Police disclosure officer of that material.

6.21 The Police disclosure officer will review that material held by the Local Authority and any material previously revealed to the Police for the purposes of carrying out secondary disclosure. The Local Authority disclosure officer will arrange for the material to be available for further review by the Police disclosure officer within [ ] working days of receiving a written request. The Local Authority disclosure officer will retain a copy of the defence statement.

6.22 In the event of the Defence making an application under section 8 of the CPIA for further disclosure of material held by the Local Authority and already considered by the Police and/or the Crown Prosecution Service in the criminal proceedings, the Crown Prosecution Service will liaise with the Police and Local Authority disclosure officers prior to the hearing of the application.

6.23 Where the defence apply for a witness summons against the Local Authority for disclosure of material not in the possession of the Police or the Crown Prosecution Service, the Local Authority will inform the Police disclosure officer and the Crown Prosecution Service of the time and place of the hearing of the witness summons and the nature and grounds of such an application.

6.24 The Prosecutor has a duty to keep under continuing review the question of whether there is any unused material, which might undermine the prosecution case or might reasonably assist the defence case. The Parties recognise that they may need to review the material again if other issues become relevant during the course of the criminal proceedings.

6.25 In the event that there are no criminal proceedings, or the proceedings are discharged, or the accused is acquitted, the police and/or Crown Prosecution Service will return all material in their possession belonging to the Local Authority.

7. Schools and other organisations involved in the care of children

7.1 Where the Police investigating a suspected crime believe material exists with Schools the Police should contact the Local Authority to identify the status of the school. Where the Local Authority identifies the school as an Independent School, it should inform the police, so that the police may approach the school directly to obtain the material.

7.2 The Parties to this protocol would encourage other organisations that are involved in the care of children, to follow the provisions laid down in this protocol in the sharing of information with the Police and Crown Prosecution Service in criminal proceedings.

8. Miscellaneous provisions

8.1 In some cases to which this protocol applies a child concerned may be (or have been) the subject of court proceedings in the family jurisdiction. Nothing in this protocol authorises the disclosure of any document filed with the court in such proceedings or any information relating to them. This applies whether the proceedings are concluded or still pending. If material is identified that falls into this category then leave must be obtained from the court in which the family proceedings are being (or were) conducted.

8.2 This draft protocol does not diminish the existing legal rights of the Parties. Specifically, it will not operate to restrict the right of any Party to claim public interest immunity in connection with any material which has come within the ambit of the police investigation.

8.3 All signatories to this protocol accept that the protocol is entered into in good faith and on that basis all signatories will use their best endeavours to comply with their terms and the spirit of the protocol.

8.4 Effect should be given to this protocol locally by a suitable service level agreement between the Parties, and any other organisation that the Parties think appropriate.

8.5   Any disagreement over the workings of this protocol or local arrangements will be referred to the agreed level of management for early and
informal resolution, wherever possible.

8.6   The Parties will at an agreed interval, monitor the workings of this protocol and any local agreement with a view to improving the efficiency and
the well being of local professional working arrangements.

ANNEX A: LEGAL FRAMEWORK

Introduction

1.   Professionals can only work together effectively to protect children if
there is an exchange of relevant information between them. This has been
recognised by the courts. In *Re G (a minor)* [1996] 2 All ER 65 Butler
Sloss LJ said:

> 'The consequences of inter-agency co-operation is that there has to
> be a free exchange of information between social workers and police
> officers together engaged in an investigation. . . . The information
> obtained by social workers in the course of their duties is however
> confidential and covered by the umbrella of public interest immu-
> nity. . . . It can however be disclosed to fellow members of the child
> protection team engaged in the investigation of possible abuse of the
> child concerned.'

2.   Any disclosure of personal information to others must always have
regard to both common law and statute law. This framework sets out the
legal position of the local authority, police and the Crown Prosecution
Service in relation to exchanging and sharing of information.

The common law of confidentiality

3.   Personal information about children and families held by the agencies is
subject to the legal duty of confidence, and should not normally be disclosed without the consent of the subject. The law permits the disclosure
of confidential information where a countervailing public interest can be
identified. Such a public interest might relate to the proper administration of justice and to the prevention of wrongdoing. The court in *R v
Chief Constable of North Wales Police, ex parte Thorpe* [1996] QB 396
Lord Bingham CJ considered that where a public body acquires information relating to a member of the public which is not generally available
and is potentially damaging, the body ought not to disclose such information save for the purpose of and to the extent necessary for performance of its public duty or enabling some other public body to perform its
public duty.

4. There is a public interest in the prevention and detection of crime and in the apprehension or prosecution of offenders. Both domestic case law and the Data Protection Act 1998 recognise that it may be necessary for a local social services authority or education authority to disclose confidential material in its possession to the police for the purposes of a police investigation or criminal proceedings. The material to be disclosed must be both relevant and necessary for the purposes of the police investigation.

5. The information the Parties to this protocol possess will have usually come to the local authority from the individual him/herself and a range of other sources. There is no publication to any member of the public. The purpose of disclosure is to facilitate the more effective administration of justice, either by providing further evidence of criminal conduct or by revealing the hopelessness of cases that might otherwise have reached the trial stage. Therefore, disclosure of material between the Parties to this protocol is permitted both by the general law on confidentiality and in particular by the law governing such disclosures by public bodies.

6. It is acknowledged that the law in the disclosure of confidential information is complex. There are restrictions on the sharing of information between the parties under the Data Protection Act and the Human Rights Act. However, the sharing of information is not necessarily contrary to these Acts.

Data Protection Act 1998

7. The Data Protection Act 1998 (the 1998 Act) requires that personal information is obtained and processed fairly and lawfully; only disclosed in appropriate circumstances; is accurate, relevant and not held longer than necessary; and is kept securely. The Act allows for disclosure without the consent of the subject in certain conditions, including for the purposes of the prevention or detection of crime, or the apprehension or prosecution of offenders, and where failure to disclose would be likely to prejudice those objectives in a particular case.

8. When disclosing personal information, many of the data protection issues surrounding disclosure can be avoided if the consent of the individual has been sought and obtained. Where consent of the individual is not sought, or is sought but withheld, there can be an exchange of information between the Parties where there is an overriding public interest or justification for doing so. The Act contains general non-disclosure provisions, but sections 27–31 provide a number of specific exemptions. Section 29 covers crime. In the context of social services and education material, personal data processed for the purposes of prevention or detection of crime and the apprehension or prosecution of offenders is exempt from the first data principle (except to the extent to which it complies with the requirements of the second and third schedules of the 1998 Act).

9. Section 35 of the 1998 Act allows for disclosure by exempting data from the non-disclosure provisions (except to the extent to which it complies with the requirements of the second and third schedules of the 1998 Act), where disclosure is required by any enactment, rule of law, or an order of the court and, where disclosure is necessary for the purpose of, or in connection with, any legal proceedings (including prospective legal proceedings), or for the purpose of obtaining legal advice or is necessary for the purposes of establishing, exercising or defending legal rights.

10. This means that the exchange of relevant information between the Parties in this protocol is not restricted under the Act because it will nearly always be the case that the exemptions constitute an overriding public interest in favour of sharing the information.

Criminal Procedure and Investigations Act 1996

11. The Criminal Procedure and Investigations Act 1996 (the 1996 Act), the Code of Practice made under section 23 of the 1996 Act, and the Attorney General's Guidelines on the disclosure of information in criminal proceedings, published November 2000, govern the disclosure of unused prosecution material to the defence. Guidance to the police and the Crown Prosecution Service is contained in the Joint Operational Instructions. The 1996 Act applies to all criminal investigations begun on or after 1 April 1997 and applies to a two-stage disclosure process. As soon as reasonably practicable after a not guilty plea in the Magistrates' Court, or service of the prosecution case, committal or transfer to the Crown Court, the prosecution must disclose to the defence any prosecution material that has not been previously disclosed and which might undermine the prosecution case (primary disclosure).

12. In Crown Court cases, the defence is required to provide, within 14 days of primary disclosure by the prosecution, a statement setting out in general terms their defence and particulars of any alibi witnesses. On receipt of the defence statement, the prosecution must as soon as reasonably practicable disclose any further material which may reasonably be expected to assist the accused's defence, as disclosed by the defence statement (secondary disclosure).

13. In Magistrates' Court cases, the defence may give a defence statement to the prosecutor. The requirements of a defence statement voluntarily given in Magistrates' Court cases are the same as those in Crown Court cases.

14. Throughout the proceedings, the prosecution is under a continuing duty to keep under review whether material should be disclosed to the defence. After the defence has provided a defence statement, the 1996 Act enables them to apply to the court for an order requiring the prosecution to disclose material if the defence considers that the prosecution has failed to comply with secondary disclosure.

15. Where the prosecution holds relevant sensitive material that meets the criteria for disclosure under the 1996 Act, then a public interest immunity application should be made to the court to withhold this material from the defence. Any decision to withhold such material is a matter for the court to determine.

16. Public interest immunity (PII) enables the courts to reconcile two conflicting public interests – the public interest in the fair administration of justice and the need to maintain the confidentiality of information the disclosure of which would be damaging to the public interest. PII is an exception to the general rule that all material which falls within the tests for disclosure must be disclosed. Special care needs to be taken in deciding where the balance lies between the two competing public interests.

17. The position of PII with respect to social services files has recently been summarised in *Re R (Care: Disclosure: Nature of Proceedings)* [2002] 1 FLR 755. Any person advancing a claim to PII in respect of material held by a local authority should set out with particularity the harm that it is alleged will be caused to the public interest. Before embarking on a claim for PII, consideration should be given to the question whether the material passes the threshold test for disclosure under the Criminal Procedure and Investigations Act 1996, and if so why.

18. The Local Authority may assert PII but it is not necessary for them to do so in every case where disclosure is sought by the prosecuting authorities and for there to be a PII hearing before the court prior to disclosure taking place.

The European Convention on Human Rights

19. The Human Rights Act 1998 gives effect to the rights and freedoms guaranteed under the European Convention on Human Rights. Article 6 ensures that every accused has the right to fair trial. It states that in the determination of his civil rights and obligations or of any criminal charge against him, everyone is entitled to a fair and public hearing within a reasonable time by an independent and impartial tribunal established by law. Article 8 protects the right to respect for private and family life, home and correspondence.

20. Article 6 is a 'special' right which means that it cannot be balanced against other public interests. On the other hand, Article 8 is a 'qualified' right which means that it can be interfered with where it is in the interests of national security, public safety or the economic well-being of the country, for the prevention of disorder or crime, for the protection of health or morals, or for the protection of the rights and freedoms of others.

21. The court will order disclosure of information regarding sexual and physical abuse of children (social service and education records) where it is necessary for an accused to have a fair trial (Article 6). The court will also order disclosure of the information where it is necessary for the protection of health or morals, for the protection of the rights and freedoms of others and for the prevention of disorder or crime (Article 8 (2)). Disclosure should be appropriate for the purpose and only to the extent necessary to achieve that purpose.

Joint investigations

22. Section 26 of the 1996 Act provides that a person other than a police officer, who is charged with a duty of conducting an investigation with a view to it being ascertained, whether a person should be charged with an offence, or whether a person charged with an offence is guilty, shall have regard to any of the provisions in the Code of Practice made under the 1996 Act. Material obtained by social services in the course of an investigation under section 47 of the Children Act 1989, which may be obtained jointly with the police, but not in the possession of the police, is not subject to section 26. However, it is acknowledged that where such material is obtained jointly with the police, the local authority should as a matter of good practice, have regard to the Code of Practice.

23. Relevant material acquired during the course of a joint investigation should be given to the police disclosure officer and listed on a sensitive or non-sensitive MG form. If there is any disagreement between the police and the local authority on the material, then this will be resolved by the Court by way of a public interest immunity application (see section 16 of the 1996 Act). Where material which has been jointly obtained is in the possession of the police, then that material is subject to the provisions of the Criminal Procedure and Investigations Act 1996.

24. In most cases social workers will be involved where the police are investigating allegations of sexual or physical abuse of children. In addition to complying with the 1996 Act, they should also adopt the Attorney General's guidelines and have regard Article 6 of the European Convention on Human Rights.

Non-joint investigations

25. Where a person subject to a criminal investigation has not been charged, it is often the case that the investigating police officer will require to know about the background of the complainant, family and associates. Such information may be helpful in assessing the veracity of any complaint and the likelihood of conviction. Occasionally, if the local authority had disclosed material to the police at an earlier stage the person under investigation would not have been charged.

26. In these circumstances, the only mechanism to enable the investigators to make application to the court for the disclosure of such material is to consider whether it is appropriate to make an application for Special Procedure Material, under Schedule 1 of the Police and Criminal Evidence Act 1984. However, this is not a satisfactory approach because it goes against the ethos and spirit of the Parties exchanging and sharing information where it is necessary to protect children.

27. Therefore, where full details of the nature of the investigation and the reasons for requiring such material are given to the local authority and that the material is treated as confidential, then it is in the interests of justice for there to be disclosure of relevant material before charge. This would be considered 'necessary' in accordance with Schedule 3 of the 1998 Act.

28. Where a person has been charged with an offence and the social services and/or education departments of a local authority have not been involved in the investigation, but holds or is believed to hold material that could be relevant, then the local authority fall within the category of a third party. The procedure for the police in obtaining such information should be in accordance with this protocol.

29. Schedule 2 of the 1998 Act allows disclosure of non-sensitive material. Such material should be listed on a non-sensitive material form which will be sent, together with the material, to the police disclosure officer who will forward it to the Crown Prosecution Service.

30. The majority of the material held by a local authority will be of a confidential nature. Where the conditions are met in Schedule 3 of the 1998 Act, material should be revealed to the police disclosure officer and the Crown Prosecution Service. The material should be listed on a sensitive material schedule and this together with the documents should be given to the police disclosure officer and the Crown Prosecution Service. Where the local authority assert public interest immunity then section 16 of the 1996 Act provides that the court must not make a disclosure order unless a person claiming an interest in the material is given the opportunity to be heard.

31. Paragraphs 30–33 of the Attorney General's Guidelines refer to material held by other agencies, which includes a local authority. If it is believed by the investigator, the police disclosure officer or the prosecutor that it is reasonable to seek production of material held by the local authority and the request is refused then application should be made for a witness summons requiring production of the material to the court. The prosecution should be pro-active in such circumstances.

Conclusion

32. The aim of the protocol is to provide an agreed framework between the Parties for the sharing and exchange of relevant material in child protection investigations. While there is a difficult balance between the local authority complying with their duty of confidentiality, and the police and the Crown Prosecution Service obtaining relevant material from the local authority at the earliest stage possible in any criminal investigation, there are no legal reasons why the Parties should not exchange the material expeditiously, as outlined in this protocol. This would benefit everyone involved in any criminal child protection investigation and promote the efficiency of the criminal justice system.

Guidance on acting in the absence of a children's guardian

NOTICE TO CHILDREN PANEL MEMBERS: REPRESENTATION OF CHILDREN IN PUBLIC LAW PROCEEDINGS

Issued by the Law Society in October 2003

Children Panel members are invited to note that the guidance contained in this notice is agreed by the Solicitors Family Law Association and the Association of Lawyers for Children.

The Law Society continues to support fully the need for a tandem model of legal representation (a solicitor and a children's guardian).

Parts of the country have, in the past, been subject to some delay between the appointment of a solicitor and the taking-up of an appointment by a guardian. We understand that sometimes considerable delay is being experienced in some regions, including in regions where such delays have not previously been experienced, and this may continue. The Society clarified in a similar notice in 2001 and 2002 what solicitors should do where a court seeks to appoint them to represent children in cases where a guardian is not immediately available.

The appointment of the solicitor for the child in care and supervision applications is dealt with by Step 1.4 of the Protocol for Judicial Case Management in Public Law Children Act Cases.

Solicitors are reminded that the decision whether or not to accept an appointment from the court to act for a child is a matter for the individual solicitor. Solicitors will be aware that their primary professional duty is to the client. In making a professional decision as to whether or not to act, the solicitor should consider whether s/he is able and competent to represent that child in accordance with the professional duty to the client. In making that professional decision, solicitors will need to have close regard to the child's best interests and vulnerability, including the urgency of the case and the impact of delay upon the child; and the age and understanding of the child.

Solicitors should carefully consider whether they will be able to act promptly and personally and whether they have sufficient experience and the appropriate expertise to equip them to deal with the particular case in the absence of a children's guardian. Solicitors are also reminded to consider making appropriate professional mentoring arrangements.

Solicitors should not refuse to accept instructions to represent a child, solely on the basis of the non-availability of a children's guardian. There is likely to be work which the solicitor can undertake in and outside of court in their role as solicitor pending the involvement of a children's guardian in order to facilitate the smooth running of the proceedings, to clarify issues and plans and to probe and test evidence.

Where the solicitor decides to act[1], s/he should conduct the proceedings in accordance with the instructions from the child where s/he is able, having regard to his/her understanding, to give such instructions. In default of instructions the solicitor should represent the child 'in furtherance of the best interests of the child' in view of Section 41 of the Children Act 1989 and Rule 4.12 of the Family Proceedings Rules 1991. What work is necessary will be a matter of professional judgment in the individual case. The solicitor should not undertake the guardian's professional role. Whilst the solicitor should act in accordance with the particular child's best interests, s/he is not in a position to advise the court what is in the child's best interests. In carrying out their professional duties the Society considers that it is proper and appropriate for children's solicitors to undertake the following tasks in the absence of a children's guardian:

- Critically appraise the local authority's actions and evidence in support of those actions, and seek a direction to require the filing of further evidence if appropriate, in order to probe and test their case and to ensure that the court has sufficient evidence on which to base its decisions; and to test the evidence of all parties at any contested interim hearing

- At every opportunity to seek the appointment of a children's guardian by CAFCASS and to keep the issue of the non-appointment of a children's guardian under constant review[2] (the matter should be brought back before the court as quickly as possible after the first hearing and be an issue for every hearing)

The appointment of the Solicitor for the Child in Care and Supervision Applications is dealt with by Step 1.4 of the Protocol for Judicial Case Management in Public Law Children Act Cases.

1   Solicitors are reminded of the Law Society Children Panel Undertaking attached [see Appendix 9] which must be complied with in all cases, whether a children's guardian is appointed or not. Continuity and consistency of representation for the child will be particularly important where no children's guardian is involved in the case.
2   The Society suggests that the solicitor put to the clerk at the outset of the case a view on the level of priority for appointment of a children's guardian by CAFCASS. In formulating this advice the solicitor may wish to consider, together with the other parties, whether in the particular case there are urgent decisions to be made on any of the following issues:

- separation and placement;
- the removal or return of the child including initial risk assessment;
- the separation of siblings;
- the need for immediate expert evidence on causation;
- the type of placement.

- To request and collate as soon as possible all relevant papers including copies from the local authority social services' records of all case conference minutes and medical or other reports relating to the child. The local authority party is likely to agree to provide to solicitors those key documents which would be disclosed in the ordinary process of discovery. However, solicitors should be aware that they have no statutory right of access to local authority records, which children's guardians have under Section 42 of the Children Act 1989, meaning that local authorities are required to comply with data protection legislation. Solicitors are encouraged to discuss with the local authority party a consensual way forward

- To be generally aware of and play a leading role in case management and time tabling issues for the benefit of the running of the proceedings as a whole, aspects of which are highlighted amongst the tasks listed below

- To consider the need for and make an application for transfer to the care centre on the basis of the best information available, considering whether this is appropriate on the usual criteria

- To attempt to see the child as soon as possible (and if possible before the first hearing) in the most appropriate setting and style for such a meeting, to ascertain any wishes and feelings of the child where it is possible for the solicitor to do so, and to ascertain whether the child's understanding is such that s/he is able to give her/his own instructions

- To report to the court any wishes and feelings of the child which the solicitor has been able to ascertain

- To attend case conferences and reviews with or on behalf of the child

- To consider seeking directions for the filing of parents' statements, together with those of any other relevant party

- To consider the issue of joinder of additional parties

- To identify and consider whether to interview any witnesses

- To consider the need for medical/psychiatric or other expert assessments and evidence, having regard in particular to the competence of the child to give instructions. It is however likely to be difficult to take an initiative on this point without instructions from a guardian, but the solicitor can identify issues where it might be more appropriate for the local authority or parents to consider instructing an expert, respond to suggestions by others and play a role in clarifying instructions and approving draft letters of instruction and time tabling

- To consider whether a split hearing is necessary

- To consider whether or not to appeal any court adjudication

Generally solicitors are recommended to be familiar with the SFLA *Guide to Good Practice for Solicitors Acting for Children* (6th Edition 2002). In particular, solicitors should have regard to Articles 6 (the right to fair trial) and 8 (the right to respect for family life) of the European Convention on Human Rights, enshrined in the law by the Human Rights Act 1998, and ensure that when acting for a child that the proceedings are conducted with due regard to such rights.

In the continuing absence of a guardian in the case, despite the solicitor contacting CAFCASS to seek the appointment of a guardian, and where the solicitor considers that urgent welfare expertise is required in the particular circumstances of the case the solicitor should apply to the court for leave to instruct an expert social worker or other appropriate expert to provide the necessary report.

Solicitors should continue to self-assess their suitability after accepting an appointment from the court to act for a child. It is a requirement of Children Panel membership that practitioners do not continue with cases which are outside their expertise. Solicitors must also be alert and sensitive to whether there is in fact a good specific reason for the particular child to:

- be represented by a solicitor of the other gender;
- be represented by a solicitor of the same ethnic background or culture as the child;
- not be represented by a solicitor with the particular ethnic background or culture of the appointed solicitor;
- be represented by someone with different specific knowledge and skills relevant to the particular case or the particular child.

The Law Society's Children Panel undertaking

I undertake that, when representing a party in proceedings covered by the Children Act 1989:

1. Subject to paragraph 2, I will not normally delegate the preparation, supervision, conduct or presentation of the case, but will deal with it personally.

2. In each case I will consider whether it is in the best interests of my client to instruct another advocate in relation to the presentation or preparation of the case.

3. If it is in the best interests of my client, or necessary, to instruct another advocate:

    3.1 I will consider and advise my client or the Children's Guardian (if applicable) who should be instructed in the best interest of my client;

    3.2 I agree that, save in exceptional circumstances, any advocate that is instructed will either be:

    (a) another Children Panel member (approved as a Children Representative if my client is the child); or

    (b) a member of the Bar on my Practices approved Counsel list.

    3.3 I will obtain an undertaking from that advocate to

    (a) attend and conduct the matter personally unless an unavoidable professional engagement arises;

    (b) take all reasonable steps to ensure that so far as reasonably practicable a conflicting professional engagement does not arise.

Signed   ....   Date   ....

Name in block capitals   ....

Law Society and CAFCASS guidance on the working relationship between Children Panel solicitors and children's guardians

Issued by the Law Society's Children Law Sub-Committee and CAFCASS

INTRODUCTION

This Guidance is intended to clarify aspects of the professional working relationship between Children Panel solicitors and children's guardians when working together to represent a child or young person within the context of public law children and adoption proceedings. It contains guidance for Children Panel solicitors and guidance for children's guardians.

This Guidance relates to the situation where the solicitor is instructed by the children's guardian on the child or young person's behalf. It does not seek to cover the situation where the solicitor is directly instructed by the child or young person.

This Guidance replaces but reflects and builds on the Protocol for the Working Relationship between Children Panel solicitors and Guardians ad Litem issued by the Law Society's Children Law Sub-Committee in conjunction with the National Association of Guardians ad Litem and Reporting Officers (NAGALRO) and the Association of Guardians ad Litem and Reporting Officers Panel Managers (AGOLROPM) in March 2000.

This Guidance should be read in conjunction with Part 4 of Good Practice in Child Care Cases published by the Law Society.

Aims of the Guidance

This Guidance is intended to provide a framework for good practice for, and good working relationships between, solicitors and children's guardians and has a number of aims:

- To remind solicitors of their role and obligations when instructed by children's guardians on behalf of a child or young person and to clarify the practice roles of each

- To assist solicitors to standardise the way in which they will offer their professional services when instructed by children's guardians
- To encourage consistent good practice for the working relationship between solicitors and children's guardians
- To encourage professional openness between solicitors and children's guardians
- To improve their working relationship and communications by codifying what solicitors and children's guardians can expect from each other
- To enhance the standard of professional service a child or young person receives by improving the working relationship between solicitors and children's guardians
- To allow for greater understanding by parents, their legal advisers and others of the practical working relationship between solicitors and children's guardians.

Status of this Guidance

This is a guide to good practice for and designed to clarify and enhance the working relationship between Children Panel solicitors and children's guardians on a national basis, with a view to standardising the expectations each may have of the other.

Children Panel Solicitors

Children Panel solicitors are, in the performance of their professional duties, subject to statute, court rules, orders of the court, rules and principles of professional conduct and the conditions of membership of the Law Society's Children Panel.

This Guidance for Children Panel solicitors is not intended to replace any of those rules or obligations.

Children's guardians

Children's guardians have a specific statutory basis for their work and are, in the performance of their professional duties, subject to court rules, orders of the court and CAFCASS Principles and Standards.

This Guidance for children's guardians is not intended to replace any of those rules or obligations.

GUIDANCE FOR CHILDREN PANEL SOLICITORS

Professional practice

1. To respond promptly to a request by a children's guardian to act for a child or young person, including when declining to act.

2. To be professional in all dealings with the children's guardian, the child or young person and other persons involved in the case and to promote the independent role of the children's guardian within the context of the court proceedings.

3. To remind the children's guardian, if necessary, about the need for the children's guardian to be, and be seen to be, both open minded and even handed.

4. To provide competent representation for the child or young person.

5. To keep under review and discuss with the children's guardian the need to avoid delay, having in mind Section 1(2) Children Act 1989; and the purpose and overriding objective of the Practice Direction (Care Cases: Judicial Continuity and Judicial Case Management) [2003] and the Protocol for Judicial Case Management in Public Law Children Act Cases (The Protocol).

6. To comply with the terms of Children Panel solicitors' personal undertakings in relation to all aspects of the case; to discuss and agree with the children's guardian substitution of advocates for hearings where the instructed solicitor is not available; to discuss with the children's guardian selection of counsel where it is necessary or desirable to instruct counsel and this has been agreed by the children's guardian.

7. To ensure that, where counsel is instructed, counsel is fully briefed including for the purposes of the Case Management Conference and Pre-Hearing Review and is provided with copies of all relevant documents. Where it is necessary to arrange a conference with counsel this should be sufficiently in advance of the Final Hearing to provide time to allow any outstanding matters to be dealt with by the solicitor or children's guardian.

8. To recognise the limits of her/his own experience and expertise and to seek advice from mentors in and outside their firm or advise a change of solicitor as necessary.

Involvement with children

9. To remember that the child or young person is the solicitor's client including where instructions are taken from the children's guardian.

10. To see the child or young person personally unless in consultation with the children's guardian the solicitor believes this would be inappropriate in the particular circumstances of the case. To consult with the

children's guardian as to the appropriate time(s) for this; to seek guidance from children's guardians on issues of age and understanding of the child or young person; to discuss with the children's guardian any issues of disclosure of information and/or documents to the child or young person.

11. To keep under review and discuss with the children's guardian the possibility that a child or young person may wish to give, and be capable of giving, separate instructions.

12. To consult with the children's guardian about the attendance of the child or young person at court hearings.

13. To consider involving the child or young person, if of sufficient age and understanding, in the selection of counsel where relevant.

14. To discuss with the children's guardian and agree the best way of advising the child or young person of the outcome of important meetings and hearings.

Documents and communication

15. At the outset of the case, to discuss and clarify with the children's guardian the roles and expectations of both solicitor and children's guardian including expectations about frequency of liaison and discussion including expectations about out of hours contact. To confirm the children's guardian's address for receipt of mail. To exchange with the children's guardian, where appropriate and requested, out of hours telephone numbers, out of hours email addresses, mobile telephone numbers and fax numbers to improve communication.

16. To discuss and agree a division of tasks and plan of work which is appropriate to the case, to provide a case plan where appropriate and to consider attendance at relevant meetings including child protection conferences.

17. To confirm that the children's guardian has accessed and read the social work files and to consider together the issue of disclosure.

18. To discuss with the children's guardian what evidence should be obtained on behalf of the child or young person, by whom and whether any interviews need to be conducted jointly.

19. To ensure that the children's guardian receives copy documents filed in the proceedings and all other relevant copy documents and correspondence.

20. To confirm that the children's guardian has a written record of all communications with the relevant Social Services Department and other persons involved in the case.

21. To liaise with the children's guardian on the content of communications with other parties.

22.   To provide any practical assistance to the children's guardian as may be necessary i.e. copying, fax and telephone facilities or office accommodation for interviews with parents etc. where practical or where safety issues arise.

23.   To anticipate any planned absence of solicitor or children's guardian and to discuss arrangements to cover any planned or unplanned absence.

24.   To be sensitive throughout to the importance of the working relationship between solicitor and children's guardian and to give and receive constructive feedback.

Legal advice to children's guardians

25.   To provide prompt, timely and well informed legal advice, assistance and support to the children's guardian.

26.   To advise on the evidence in terms of any gaps or lack of clarity in the evidence or evidence identified contrary to the children's guardian's view.

27.   To provide advice about whether expert evidence is necessary and to seek agreement to all letters of instruction to expert witnesses and others commissioned by or on behalf of the children's guardian or draft letters of instruction prepared by other parties' legal representatives.

28.   To remind the children's guardian of the provisions in The Protocol as necessary particularly in relation to local practice.

29.   To prepare and provide any documents as required for the assistance of the court, other parties and children's guardian including, for example:

- Case Synopsis
- Case Management Documents
- Statements of Evidence
- Draft Directions and Orders
- Schedule of Issues.

30.   To liaise with the children's guardian in relation to the preparation for the final hearing and to consider and advise on legal and factual issues relevant to the formulation of recommendations as to available options including discussion and advice on presentation of evidence and draft reports. To advise the children's guardian that the solicitor generally needs to see the children's guardian's draft report in time for the hearing, certainly where the case is difficult or the children's guardian is inexperienced, in order for the solicitor to confirm that, for example, the report covers all necessary information, identifies any sources of hearsay, reflects the law correctly, and is properly balanced in its assessment and recommendations.

31. To provide advice as to relevant legal developments and case law changes affecting the relevant issues to the proceedings and to assist the children's guardian in negotiations throughout the course of the proceedings.

32. To prepare the children's guardian for evidence in chief and cross-examination prior to the hearing.

33. To discuss and review the case with the children's guardian upon completion and to provide the children's guardian with a note of the judgment and, where appropriate, advise on appeal.

GUIDANCE FOR CHILDREN'S GUARDIANS

Professional practice

1. To appoint a solicitor promptly to represent the child or young person; or, when allocated the matter after the solicitor's appointment, to consider whether (in accordance with paragraph 12 of the Statement of Good Practice in the Appointment of Solicitors for Children where it falls to the Court to do so in Specified Proceedings accompanying The Protocol) it is in the best interests of the child or young person for the solicitor to continue acting.

2. To be professional in all dealings with solicitors and other persons involved in the case.

3. To be, and be seen to be, both open minded and even handed.

4. To keep clear records of all plans, contemporaneous notes of interviews and other documentation acquired throughout the investigation.

5. To keep under review and discuss with the solicitor the need to avoid delay, having in mind Section 1(2) Children Act 1989 and The Protocol.

6. To attend all hearings unless excused by the court.

7. To consider, with the solicitor, all the evidence. To form a view, which may change during the course of proceedings, informed by all the relevant evidence.

8. To recognise the limits of her/his own expertise and in consultation with the solicitor to seek expert advice where necessary, taking into account Appendix C of The Protocol.

Involvement with children

9. To recognise that the child or young person is the solicitor's client and that the solicitor, unlike the children's guardian, owes a duty of confidentiality to the child or young person.

10. To advise the solicitor about issues of age and understanding of a child or young person and to accept the judgement of the solicitor in accordance with the professional conduct guidance as to the capacity of the child or young person to give instructions. To advise the solicitor about any issue of disclosure of information and/or documents to the child or young person where appropriate.

11. To advise the solicitor about the attendance of the child or young person at court hearings.

12. To provide informed advice to the solicitor about issues of child development, social work practice and procedure and relevant research.

13. To discuss with the solicitor and agree the best way of advising the child or young person of the outcome.

Documents and communication

14. To discuss and clarify with the solicitor the roles and expectations of both solicitor and children's guardian at the outset of the case including expectations about frequency of liaison and discussion including expectations about out of hours contact. To confirm to the solicitor the address for receipt of mail. To discuss with the solicitor the need for exchange of out of hours telephone numbers, out of hours email addresses, mobile telephone numbers and fax numbers in certain circumstances.

15. To discuss and agree a division of tasks and plan of work with the solicitor which is appropriate to the case, to discuss the case plan with the solicitor and to discuss with the solicitor any requirement for attendance at child protection conferences, reviews and planning or other relevant meetings.

16. To recognise the importance of discussing with the solicitor their reports in draft form prior to submission to the court in relation to the legal and factual issues relevant to the formulation of recommendations.

17. To anticipate any planned absence of solicitor or children's guardian and to discuss arrangements to cover any planned or unplanned absence.

18. To be sensitive throughout to the importance of the working relationship between solicitor and children's guardian and to give and receive constructive feedback.

Instructions to solicitors

19. To liaise closely with the solicitor and provide timely instructions throughout the case including for all court hearings and relevant meetings.

20. To discuss with the solicitor what evidence should be obtained, by whom and whether any interviews need to be conducted jointly.

21. To address on a continuing basis issues relevant to the particular court proceedings, duties under the court rules and to the welfare of the child or young person within these.

22. To discuss and review the case with the solicitor upon completion and, where appropriate, discuss appeal.

APPENDIX 11

Useful contacts and websites

Association of Lawyers for Children (ALC)
PO Box 283
East Molesey
Surrey KT8 OWH
Tel/Fax: 020 8224 7071
E-mail: admin@alc.org.uk
www.alc.org.uk

The Law Society (general enquiries)
113 Chancery Lane
London WC2A 1PL
Tel: 020 7242 1222
DX: 56 London/Chancery Lane
www.lawsociety.org.uk

Practice Advice Service (matters of legal practice and procedure)
The Law Society
Library and Information Services
113 Chancery Lane
London WC2A 1PL
DX 56 London/Chancery Lane
Tel: 0870 606 2522
Fax: 020 7316 5541
E-mail: lib-pas@lawsociety.org.uk

Law Society's Children Panel
The Law Society
Ipsley Court
Berrington Close
Redditch
Worcs B98 OTD
Tel: 0870 606 2555
E-mail: panels@lawsociety.org.uk
www.panels.lawsociety.org.uk

Office of the Official Solicitor
81 Chancery Lane
London WC2A 1DD
Tel: 020 7911 7127
E-mail: enquiries@offsol.gsi.gov.uk
www.offsol.demon.co.uk

Professional Ethics (issues of professional conduct)
The Law Society
Ipsley Court
Redditch
Worcs B98 OTD
Tel: 0870 606 2577
www.guide-on-line.lawsociety.org.uk

Solicitors Family Law Association (SFLA)
PO Box 302
Orpington, Kent
BR6 8QX
Tel: 01689 850227
Fax: 01689 855833
DX 86853 Locksbottom
E-mail: info@sfla.org.uk
www.sfla.org.uk

Other useful websites include:

CAFCASS
www.cafcass.gov.uk

Carelaw: 'A Guide to the Law for Young People in Care' (NCH and SFLA)
www.carelaw.org.uk

Court Service: for 'Protocol for Judicial Case Management in Public Law Children Act Cases', forms and guidance and 'Adoption Proceedings – a New Approach'
www.courtservice.gov.uk/using_courts/protocol/index.htm
www.courtservice.gov.uk/using_courts/guides_notices/notices/family/president.htm
www.courtservice.gov.uk/cms/forms.htm
www.courtservice.gov.uk/cms/media/a20b.pdf

Department of Health: adoption information
www.doh.gov.uk/adoption
www.doh.gov.uk/adoption/links.htm

Family Rights Group
www.frg.org.uk

Legal Services Commission
www.legalservices.gov.uk

NAGALRO
www.nagalro.com

NCH: 'Its Not Your Fault' guide for children
www.itsnotyourfault.org.uk

NSPCC
www.nspcc.org.uk
www.nspcc.org.uk/inform

Office of the High Commissioner for Human Rights
www.unhchr.ch

Index

Understanding Legal Aid

A Practical Guide to Public Funding

Vicky Ling and
Simon Pugh

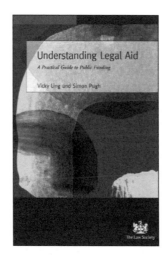

This is a quick reference guide to
the various types of public funding
available and the context in which
they operate. The emphasis is on
the practical implementation of the
schemes and wherever possible
tactical advice and checklists are provided.

- covers both civil and criminal legal aid schemes
- provides useful insights into other services performed by the
  Legal Services Commission, such as the Community Legal
  Service and Public Defender Service
- includes cross-references to official sources of information for
  other areas.

Written by a leading consultant and a specialist practitioner,
Understanding Legal Aid is an easily comprehensible guide to
undertaking publicly funded work, applicable equally to solicitors,
the not-for-profit sector and the Bar.

Available from Marston Book Services:
Tel. 01235 465 656

1 85328 895 0
256 pages
Sept 2003
£29.95

The Law Society

Elderly Client Handbook

3rd edition

General Editors:
Caroline Bielanska & Martin Terrell
Consultant Editor:
Gordon R. Ashton

Published in association with
Solicitors for the Elderly

Advising elderly clients requires an
up-to-date knowledge of many varied
areas of law and practice. This book
provides a succinct guide to all the relevant law, together with practical
advice on the running and marketing of an elderly client practice.

It provides clear and up-to-date analysis of:
• British Banking Association's guidelines
• Mental Incapacity Bill
• Financial Services Act 2000
• Reforms to health and social care
• Care Standards Act 2000
• Changes to the Court of Protection and Public Guardianship Office
• Benefits including Pension Credit.

The third edition has been fully revised by a team of new
contributors drawn from the membership of Solicitors for the Elderly
and experts in the fields of mental capacity, mental health law and
employment law.

Available from Marston Book Services:
Tel. 01235 465 656

1 85328 872 1
520 pages
March 2004
£44.95

The Law Society